THE MULTIPLAYER CLASSROOM: DESIGNING COURSEWORK AS A GAME

LEE SHELDON

Course Technology PTR
A part of Cengage Learning

COURSE TECHNOLOGY
CENGAGE Learning

Australia • Brazil • Japan • Korea • Mexico • Singapore • Spain • United Kingdom • United States

COURSE TECHNOLOGY
CENGAGE Learning™

The Multiplayer Classroom: Designing Coursework as a Game
Lee Sheldon

Publisher and General Manager, Course Technology PTR: Stacy L. Hiquet

Associate Director of Marketing: Sarah Panella

Manager of Editorial Services: Heather Talbot

Marketing Manager: Jordan Castellani

Senior Acquisitions Editor: Emi Smith

Project and Copy Editor: Marta Justak

Interior Layout Tech: MPS Limited, a Macmillan Company

Cover Designer: Mike Tanamachi

Indexer: Valerie Haynes

Proofreader: Caroline Roop

For product information and technology assistance, contact us at **Cengage Learning Customer & Sales Support, 1-800-354-9706**

For permission to use material from this text or product, submit all requests online at **www.cengage.com/permissions** Further permissions questions can be emailed to **permissionrequest@cengage.com**

All trademarks are the property of their respective owners.

Library of Congress Control Number: 2011923931

ISBN-13: 978-1-4354-5844-4

ISBN-10: 1-4354-5844-3

Course Technology, a part of Cengage Learning
20 Channel Center Street
Boston, MA 02210
USA

Cengage Learning is a leading provider of customized learning solutions with office locations around the globe, including Singapore, the United Kingdom, Australia, Mexico, Brazil, and Japan. Locate your local office at: **international.cengage.com/region**

Cengage Learning products are represented in Canada by Nelson Education, Ltd.

For your lifelong learning solutions, visit **courseptr.com**

Visit our corporate website at **cengage.com**

Printed in the United States of America
2 3 4 5 6 7 13

For Emma and Graham

With all my love, my gentle, courageous children.

Acknowledgments

Many people helped take the multiplayer classroom from the virtual world to the real. First, I'd like to thank those who made the book possible. Jurie Horneman asked the question in the Game Design Workshop that caused me to share my syllabus with, among others, Jesse Schell. Jesse mentioned the XP instead of grades idea in his Dice talk last winter. That, and the resulting publicity, prompted educators from around the world to deluge me with questions about designing coursework as a game. Ted Castronova was an early supporter. Jenna Hoffstein set up the first blog and forums so we could share our experiences. Emi Smith at Cengage Learning allowed me to put aside another book when the *Multiplayer Classroom* demanded to be written instead. Alida Field lent an able hand with the initial research. Susan Kelly contributed her customarily amiable moral support. And finally, Marta Justak was a very, very patient editor.

The eight case histories in this book were contributed by visitors to the forums or educators who wrote to me directly to share their stories. These were Matthew Baylor (with Charles Souza), Jessica Broussard, Denishia Buchanan, Carl Creasman, David Grimes, Stacy Jacob, Max Lieberman (with Connie Hackathorn and Wayne Brent), and Aaron Pavao. I'd also like to acknowledge the efforts of Read Schuchardt and Sylvia Tiala.

Marie-Pierre Huguet, Senior Course Developer, Rensselaer Polytechnic Institute Innovation and Research in Teaching and Learning, provided support on many levels both at Rensselaer and now at the University of Connecticut, including her observations on Level 8, LMS graphics, editing both text and video, and generally terrific advice. Her Course Development Team: Alex Colello worked on the LMS websites and videotaped; Jeff Danis and Abbey Stein also contributed LMS support. Additional videotaping was provided by Xiyao Huang.

And last, but by no stretch of the imagination least, I'm delighted to extend a very special thank you to Erin Glasheen, who had both me and this project suddenly drop from the clear blue sky into the middle of her life not very long ago. She faced this disruption with support, encouragement, and faith that kept me going through what seemed at times an impossible task, even at the expense of her own writing, which I have no doubt will one day be found alongside this volume on our bookcase.

To everyone who aided and abetted this undertaking over the past year: you are all l33t hax0rs!

ABOUT THE AUTHOR

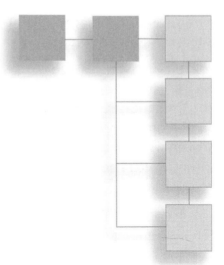

Lee Sheldon is associate professor and co-director of the Games and Simulation Arts and Sciences program at Rensselaer Polytechnic Institute. He has written and designed over 20 commercial video games and MMOs. His book *Character Development and Storytelling for Games* is required reading for many game developers and in game design programs at some of the world's most distinguished universities. A new edition will be published in 2012. Lee is a contributor to several books on video games including *Well-Played 2.0* from Carnegie-Mellon's ETC, *Writing for Video Game Genres* from the IGDA, and *Game Design: An Interactive Experience* and *Second Person*. He is cited in many publications, and he is a regular lecturer and consultant on game design and writing in the U.S. and abroad.

Before his career in video games, Lee wrote and produced over 200 popular television shows, including *Star Trek: The Next Generation* and *Charlie's Angels*. As head writer of the daytime serial *Edge of Night*, he received a nomination for best writing from the Writers Guild of America. Lee has been nominated twice for Edgar Awards by the Mystery Writers of America. His first mystery novel, *Impossible Bliss*, was reissued in 2004.

Lee began his academic career in 2006 at Indiana University where he taught game design and screenwriting. At IU, Lee first instituted the practice of designing classes as multiplayer games; worked on the serious games *Quest Atlantis* and *Virtual Congress*; and wrote and designed the alternate reality games, *The Skeleton Chase* and *Skeleton Chase 2: The Psychic*, funded by the Robert Wood Johnson Foundation; and *Skeleton Chase 3: Warp Speed* funded by

Coca-Cola. He continues as creative director of the narrative-driven MMO *Londontown*, and he is head of the team working to build the Emergent Reality Lab at Rensselaer. He is also design consultant and lead writer on the upcoming casual MMO, *Star Trek: Infinite Space*.

Contents

INTRODUCTION

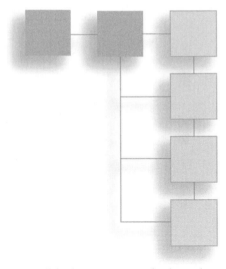

If you have picked up this book with the idea that it will help you to include video games in your curriculum, put it down now. Walk away. There is nothing to see here (as Figure I.1 so aptly demonstrates).

Figure I.1
No video games to buy here

The multiplayer classroom *is* a game. It can be created without buying software. It can be played without computers. If teachers have never played a video game in their lives, they can create a course as a multiplayer classroom.

As you will see, the multiplayer classroom is not just for teaching about games. The number of different subjects that can be taught at any grade level from elementary school to graduate school has yet to be determined. Will it work for every subject? Will it work outside traditional classrooms in the corporate world or government? There is no reason *not* to think so. All we need to do is try.

The terminology used in this book, while familiar to professional game developers, may not be as familiar to educators, even those who may have introduced a video game into a class or grown up playing them. So, with apologies to my sister and brother game designers, I'm going to define the terminology we use on a daily basis to ensure that we are all on the same page.

Definitions

I will separate these definitions like this throughout the text to spare readers from having to continually look for the meaning of a word far removed from its context. We will both figuratively and literally remain on the same page.

One way in which playing video games and traditional learning practices differ is in how they treat mistakes. Mistakes are most often punished, and busy teachers do not always have time to mark the correct answer on an exam or a paper. So students only know when they've gotten something wrong. This tends to focus their attention more on grades than on content.

We have all heard the expression "learning from your mistakes." In video games, the primary way that players learn is from making mistakes. They try something, say crossing a chasm by leaping, and their avatar falls in instead. Then their avatar magically resurrects! Now they can try using the bridge. In the end, they will figure out how to cross that chasm. And they will be rewarded for their success by the emotion "fiero" and not punished for their failures.

Fiero

Fiero is an Italian word meaning "pride," borrowed by Nicole Lazzaro and Hal Barwood to describe an immediate feeling of exhilaration triggered by personal triumph over adversity.

Because the consequences are seldom as harsh as failing an exam, players simply try again and again until they figure out how to solve the problem. During complex multiplayer boss raids, dedicated players may work for weeks to discover the correct strategy to be victorious in a single battle, even if they are supported by mentors who have cracked the problem or online hints.

Boss Raid

A boss raid is an attack by multiple players on a particularly difficult opponent, usually the "boss" of an entire area of a game.

If you have noticed that your students appear to be more focused on their successful guild raid last night in an MMO like *World of Warcraft*, or the productivity of their city in *Cityville*, than they are on their homework assignments, and have wondered how to direct an equally intense focus onto their schoolwork, take this lesson to heart. It is one of the reasons the multiplayer classroom seems to work so well.

MMO: Massively-Multiplayer Online

An MMO is a game played over the Internet by many players in any part of the world. MMO is a shortened version of MMOG (Massively Multiplayer Online Game), which is a shortened version of MMORPG (Massively Multiplayer Online Role-Playing Game). It is a type of game still in search of a reasonable acronym. Since my first classroom game would be played by no more than 40 students, the word "massively" doesn't really apply. Since it was played in the real world instead of over the Internet, the word "online" is out of place as well. That would leave me with the totally useless acronym of "M," so I'm adding a "C" and calling it a *multiplayer classroom.*

I have made plenty of mistakes along the way. So have others beginning to use the multiplayer classroom. And I'm sure I will make many more. I do not intend to hide those mistakes. In fact, much like those intrepid volunteers in the dunking tank at school fairs, my falls from grace will be in plain view. In this way, hopefully, you can avoid your own. Look for them. They'll be impossible to miss.

In September of 2009, I had no idea I would be compelled to write a book called *The Multiplayer Classroom*. I was teaching my first class as a multiplayer game in the style of a commercial MMO.

As that semester progressed, I began to see the fun of learning the students were experiencing *and how much more fun teaching* felt to me. When grades improved and class attendance headed toward a record high, I began to ask myself, "Why haven't we been designing classes as games for a long time now?"

After all, anyone born after the mid-1970s is of the gamer generation in the same way I was of the television generation. They grew up with video games already established as viable commercial products and as products capable of teaching. When they were ready to go online, the Internet magically appeared. When they wanted to expand their social networking, Facebook arrived. And when they

Figure I.2
"Beyond Facebook: The Future of Pervasive Games."

wanted to carry their games in their pockets and purses along with their cell phone and an Internet connection, the iPhone made what was already possible . . . fun.

This generation sees games all around them. As Jesse Schell points out in his talk, "Beyond Facebook: The Future of Pervasive Games," there are games everywhere we turn (see Figure I.2).

The gamer generation is part of a society used to collecting airline mileage points and open table dining points in the same way they collected gold stars in kindergarten. We'll talk more about extrinsic versus intrinsic rewards later. The point here is simply that the gamer generation takes these things in stride. They expect it—even if they aren't hard-core video gamers themselves.

Pervasive Game

A pervasive game is a game where the line between the game and reality blurs to the point where it is difficult to distinguish one from the other.

The awareness of the impact of video games on students has not been lost on educators, but much like the first stumbling attempts to integrate story into games, the first attempts to integrate games into the classroom have not been a resounding success. From here, it looks a lot like missing the forest because of all those trees in the way.

What got me to this point? Why was I personally moved to design a class as a game?

I started out in Hollywood and New York writing and producing television. In 1982, I was preparing to write a pilot for a potential TV series that involved a family able to travel through video games on their big screen TV to other planes of existence. I had never played a video game in my life. Interested in collaboration, the production companies involved, Tomorrow Entertainment and Procter & Gamble, sent me to Atari, the most successful maker of video games at that time, to learn more about them.

Their game console, the 2600, was a runaway success. They gave me one and a stack of games to play. In the interest of research, I decided to give them a try.

That TV show was never made, but soon after, using a dedicated word processor on a TV show I wrote for called *Tucker's Witch*, I bought my first IBM PC, word processing software, and a handful of the first computer games including *Microsoft Adventure*, a rebranded text adventure originally known as *Colossal Cave*, and *Ulysses and the Golden Fleece*, another adventure with graphics and a rather jumbled view of mythology!

In 1994, I turned my back on television and became a professional game writer and designer. In 2006, while still making commercial video games, I accepted a position as an assistant professor at Indiana University, teaching students how to make them.

One other significant event occurred at IU. I designed a series of Alternate Reality Games: *The Skeleton Chase, Skeleton Chase 2: The Psychic* (Figure I.3), and *Skeleton Chase 3: Warp Speed*.

Alternate Reality Game (ARG)

An ARG is a type of pervasive game that uses the real world as a platform, often involving multiple media and game elements, to tell a story that may be affected by participants' ideas or actions.

Figure I.3
Skeleton Chase 2: The Psychic.

The first two were funded by a grant from the Robert Wood Johnson Foundation. The third was funded by Coca-Cola. For the RWJ grant, we tested the efficacy of using a game as a fitness intervention. For two seven-week periods, we ran students all over the campus and surrounding town of Bloomington.

For *Skeleton Chase 3: Warp Speed,* I compressed the seven weeks of gameplay from the second game into two-and-a-half days to provide an engaging new approach to team building and learning new technologies for Coca-Cola executives from North Africa.

The designing and running of these games taught me two important lessons:

- Games as compelling as videogames can be designed to be played in the real world.

- Games played in the real world in real time demand a tremendous flexibility. You can't program real people to do what you want them to do in the same way you can program NPCs in a video game, and you can't depend on bending things like the weather to match your design. You must be ready for all the little surprises real life can throw at you and write and design on the fly.

I think the experience with the Alternate Reality Games, the last of which concluded the summer I began designing my first class as a game, is what finally made me realize that since anywhere can be a game board, why not a classroom?

And if you are going to teach a class about game design, why not design it as a game? Two! Two layers of learning in one package! Come to think of it, if you are going to write a book about designing a class as a game, why not design that book as a game as well?

So, turn the page. You will start where the player's avatar always starts—at Level 1.

COMPANION BLOG

You can find a companion blog to the book at *http://gamingtheclassroom. wordpress.com/*.

SECTION ONE

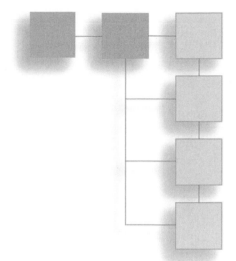

INTRODUCTION

"Good Morning. You All Have an F."

"Good morning. Welcome to the first class of the semester. Everyone in this class is going to receive an F."

One thing I will always regret when I look back on that first day of a new way of teaching is that I didn't have somebody with a camera standing by to record the expressions on the students' faces. The mixture of disbelief, shock, fear, growing umbrage, and more was something to behold.

I had a fleeting thought: What if . . . what if I just walked out after delivering that first line?

At this, the beginning of my third year in the halls of academe, I still wasn't certain I wanted to be a college professor. There was much to like about the job. My colleagues first and foremost; the intellectual engagement and discussion (something that wasn't always available during my years in Hollywood); the opportunities for me to learn; and the Bloomington campus of Indiana University itself, regarded as one of the most beautiful in the country and rightly so.

My office looked over the Arboretum (see Figure 1.1), the green expanse of grass, gurgling stream, trees and flowers crisscrossed by walkways at the heart of the campus. To my right was Wells Library. Beyond the Arboretum loomed more monolithic buildings built with the limestone that region of southern Indiana is noted for. The bucolic scene that often captured my attention was once the university's stadium, the site of the Little 500 bicycle race featured in the film *Breaking Away*.

Figure 1.1
Indiana University Arboretum.

Not only did the Arboretum welcome my woolgathering when I turned bleary-eyed from the computer to refresh both sight and mind, but it also served as a primary location in the first alternate reality game I designed while at IU. That red clock with its eclectic repertoire of chimes, those stone gazebos, bronze statuary—all would take on greater significance in the story of mystery and mayhem we told. More about that later.

Not all aspects of college life were welcome to this refugee from the real world. The bureaucracy can grind as slowly as a limestone wheel, at times crushing ideas and new initiatives beneath its weight. Faculty meetings at times reduced my reasonable, intelligent, witty human colleagues to priests droning in what seemed like a dead language with arcane rituals only the academy understands. And, of course, grading. Grading. I'm haunted by the first class I ever taught at IU; that attempt at grading where I gave letter grades based not on percentages, but feelings, and then tried desperately to translate them into real numbers. My poor students. The tears. The horror.

I didn't walk out after announcing everyone had an F that first day of a class. Although some students might disagree, I'm not quite that sadistic. Instead, I continued, "Unless..."

... they embarked on quests, defeated mobs, and crafted goods from raw materials that would help them earn their way through the brave new world they had just entered. It might look like a classroom, but it was not. And what they experienced there would count, just as it did in a video game. They could level up. Even to an A.

There was an immediate and perceptible shift in the room from shock to interest, and something more: challenge. The gauntlet was thrown right back at me.

Mob

Mob is short for "mobile," the word coined by Richard Bartle, along with Roy Trubshaw, the two creators of the first MUD (multi-user dungeon), the precursor to today's MMOs. It means any NPC (non-player character) opponent controlled by the computer, rather than another player in an MMO.

OPENING: THE SLIDE

The DICE Summit is held once a year by the Academy of Interactive Arts and Sciences to recognize outstanding achievements and contributions in the gaming industry. As Bryan Ma described it in a later Gamasutra article, Professor Jesse Schell's talk "starts on the topic of the rise of social media games and moves to discussing convergence of social/new media, technology, entertainment, and so on through game-like constructs, essentially, gameplay being incorporated into everything else we do." The gamification of society that had been going on underground for years suddenly became a hot topic with this one talk. And much to my surprise, I was participating in it.

In my case, the reference was to that class I taught at Indiana University in fall 2009, called "Theory and Practice of Game Design" (see Figure 1.2). We will examine this first iteration of the multiplayer classroom in detail when we reach Levels 3 and 4.

Lee Sheldon's Grading Procedure: You will begin on the first day of class as a Level One avatar. Level Twelve is the highest level you can achieve.

Level	XP*	Letter Grade
Level Twelve	1860	A
Level Eleven	1800	A-
Level Ten	1740	B+
Level Nine	1660	B
Level Eight	1600	B-
Level Seven	1540	C+
Level Six	1460	C
Level Five	1400	C-
Level Four	1340	D+
Level Three	1260	D
Level Two	1200	D-
Level One	0	F

Figure 1.2
He could have at least found a *good* picture of me.

Professor Schell highlighted one aspect of the class that fit the theme of his talk: my grading system used experience points, or XP, to track student progress, not letter grades. The first wave of inquiries from the press and educators hit almost immediately. A second wave struck when Professor Schell's talk was picked up as the first non-TED talk to be highlighted as part of a weekly series on their website.

Again, most of the focus was on experience points. When I began to explain that, in fact, the entire class had been designed as a multiplayer role-playing game in the vein of *World of Warcraft,* enough new questions were being asked that a graduate student of mine created a blog with attached forums to answer as many as we could: *www.gamingtheclassroom.wordpress.com.* What a number of those inquiring minds didn't realize was that we weren't playing *World of Warcraft,* or any MMO, and we had not created an island of learning within *Second Life* (see Figure 1.3).

The class *was* the game—played out in real-time in the real world of the classroom with students as players and the teacher as Game Master (see Figure 1.4).

Figure 1.3
A virtual classroom on the Ohio University *Second Life* campus.

Figure 1.4
An MMO *in* the classroom.

MIDDLE GAME: THE SHIFT

The middle game is wide open. The overall course of the game may have been charted, but here many options present themselves. The number of possible positions is great. The players have any number of decisions to make.

By the time the blog was up and running, I was in the middle of teaching a second class called "Multiplayer Game Design" for the spring 2010 semester. This class is the subject of Levels 5 and 6.

You could think of the first class as an alpha. By the second iteration, we were in closed beta. These are software development terms that mark important milestones in the development of the game that focus on testing game elements.

During the spring semester, I was also in the process of writing a book for Cengage called *Practical Game Design: A Toolkit for Educators, Researchers, and Corporations* to help nongame developers face the daunting task of creating games that have gone by a number of different designations over the years: educational games, serious games, persuasive games. Each is its own slightly different animal. My personal favorite for an umbrella term for all such endeavors is *applied games*, proposed at the 2010 Game Education Summit by Dr. Vinod Srinivasan of Texas A&M University's Department of Visualization.

Dr. Srinivasan argues convincingly that "applied" is a familiar word to us, and it has been successfully used in a number of fields. Wikipedia describes applied math as "that branch of mathematics typically used in the application of mathematical knowledge to other domains"; and science as the "application of scientific knowledge transferred into a physical environment." What are these games, if not an application of game design knowledge to other domains like education and persuasion, transferred into environments that may be physical or at least virtually physical?

There are two distinct groups of developers creating games in the rapidly expanding field of applied games. The first comprises educators, students, and businesspersons who are not familiar with basic game design and development techniques. The second group is composed of commercial game designers who are equally unfamiliar with the particular requirements of serious educational games. *Practical Game Design* was going to provide the information and tools to fund, staff, design, and develop sensible, practical, producible video games, virtual worlds, and alternate reality games. But what I came to call the *multiplayer classroom* took on a life of its own, overshadowing *Practical Game Design.*

I remember when I first proposed the idea of designing classes as games to my colleagues in the Department of Telecommunications in May of 2009. Professor Edward Castronova, an innovative teacher and economist who focuses on massively multiplayer games, had been experimenting with bringing elements of games into the classroom. He was immediately taken with the idea. But others were skeptical that such an approach might not work outside of the area of video games. Yet, as we shall see, designing classes as games has produced some very interesting results in classrooms ranging from middle school through university-level courses in a variety of disciplines. We have yet to discover a class that cannot be taught in this way. Maybe we never will.

When the interest surrounding the multiplayer classroom first appeared, I contemplated adding a chapter to *Practical Game Design.* But as the interest continued to grow, and when the second class designed as a game began to reveal a number of reasons why the approach might have merit beyond teaching video game design, I approached Cengage with the idea of writing a separate book—the one you now hold in your hands. *Practical Game Design* will have to wait for another day.

Endgame: The Book

Here you will find instruction on how to design classes as games on any subject to reach the students of today through the same methods that inspire their interest in many types of games from AAA video games to casual games on Facebook and the iPhone to alternate reality games played in real-time in the real world.

There will be specific blueprints on how to construct a multiplayer classroom. We'll explore how to approach grading as attrition, rather than focusing on letter grades, and how to tap into the social networking memes and tools already used by students. We will examine that which is unique to a particular subject or teacher, and what can be universally applied to a vast range of topics by anyone.

Case studies of both my own classes and those now being designed by other educators who are embracing the idea will provide in-depth looks at game design elements that worked and some that didn't—failures, as well as successes.

The topic is incredibly important. Today, students are struggling. They leave school with the feeling they've survived a grueling marathon instead of with an abiding thirst to continue to seek knowledge. Society is not unaware of this. Everywhere educators from K–12 to university professors are attempting to negotiate the widening gap between decades-old teaching methods and the video game-playing, social-networking students of today. This book is the first attempt to attack this challenge on its own ground: to create a new way of teaching that not only re-engages students, but also teaches them more efficiently than the standard lecture and exam grind.

We will start with efforts to bring video games and virtual worlds into the classroom as teaching tools, a literal-minded approach that has had difficulties, whether 1) existing commercial games are used, or 2) existing applied games, or 3) games designed for specific classes by outside developers or students, or 4) games designed for specific classes by those teaching them.

Research on the efficacy of all four approaches, as we shall see, is mixed in its findings. This isn't surprising. Research on the whole is quite good at measuring whether appropriate subject matter is present in a game design. It is rare, however, to find research that takes into account the quality of the game design itself.

In the four iterations of the multiplayer classroom in this book—and in the other case studies by other educators also presented here—you will see that necessary analysis at work just as it would be in the development cycle of *Uncharted 2: Among Thieves*, arguably one of the best storytelling games of 2009, or single games from the *Call of Duty*, *Grand Theft Auto*, and *Super Mario* franchises, that have grossed over a billion dollars each.

In August of 2010, I left Indiana University and headed east to become co-director of the Games and Simulation Arts and Sciences program at Rensselaer Polytechnic Institute (see Figure 1.5).

The third iteration of the multiplayer classroom, "Introduction to Game Design," was taught here during that first semester. It bore many similarities to the two classes I taught at IU. Thanks to Marie-Pierre Huguet, then Senior Course Developer, Innovation and Research in Teaching and Learning Office of Undergraduate Education, and her team, we were able to document the multiplayer classroom with video. Levels 9 and 10 cover this class, and you'll find her thoughts on the experience later in this book.

Figure 1.5
Experimental Media and Performing Arts Center at Rensselaer Polytechnic Institute.

I'm now teaching the fourth multiplayer class: "Designing Interactive Characters for Digital Games." The subject matter of this course is different enough from the first three that I've designed an entirely new game. The class is still ongoing as I write this, but it is being videoed as well. Level 10 is a record of the experience to date.

And you, gentle reader, don't simply need to be a consumer. If you apply what you learn here, or have been exploring this concept on your own, record your results. Come visit our community at *www.gamingtheclassroom.wordpress.com*. Contribute!

Of course, this isn't really the endgame. This book is unfinished. The rest of the story will be written by you.

GAMES IN THE CLASSROOM

Learning through play is not a new concept. It is the fundamental way young mammals acquire knowledge of the world around them. In both the fields of education and psychology, much research has shown that human children are no different. Their sense of the world comes into focus during early play. They develop the skills necessary to survive physically, mentally, and emotionally. And because failure in play is rarely catastrophic, they acquire the confidence necessary to try new approaches to the world around them.

Children experiment from the very first moment their senses are switched on. They smell, taste, and touch. A child will be drawn to the heat of a fire, but once burned will learn to keep her distance. The mistake has taught her more about fire than any lecturer can.

So why then once children reach a certain age do we interrupt their play? Learning becomes serious. Play is considered frivolous, at best a way to blow off a little steam. We know what happens when steam is allowed to build up without release, don't we?

Yet, we not only decide that it is time to get serious about learning, but we regiment it. Lectures become rote. Tests are standardized. Measurements become more important than knowledge. Failure is penalized with a big "F." But what are we measuring exactly? A child's ability to learn? Our ability to educate? They were doing just fine before we decided to turn them into miniature adults like those disturbing children in seventeenth and eighteenth century portraits, as shown in Figure 2.1. I realize I'm only using an analogy here, but that analogy creeps me out more than any standardized zombie invasion.

Figure 2.1
Portrait of a Child with a Coral (1636).

Who decided when to pull the switch? "Okay, enough of this learning about the world naturally. I want you to sit there, unmoving, and listen while I do your thinking for you. Memorize what I'm saying so you can take a standardized test so you can be compared to lots of other standardized children, and our school will get paid better for educating you better."

Happily, educators for years have devised their own ways of retaining a sense of play in the classroom. Even in the face of multiple choice exams, so that computers can grade for us and then compile all sorts of data full of rich mining opportunities, games sneak into the classrooms. So it shouldn't be any surprise that when video games came along, they were smuggled in as well.

EDUCATIONAL SOFTWARE

Educational software has been around a lot longer than you might think. Flight simulators date back to the 1940s. The original PLATO (Programmed Logic for Automated Teaching Operations) system was developed in 1960 at the

University of Illinois, and the last PLATO terminal was still in operation until 2006. The PLATO IV system boasted a number of features that would become common on home computers just a few years later. These included rudimentary graphics, sound, and even touchscreens.

Up until 1975, educational software systems ran on university- and government-owned mainframes, accessed by terminals. They were very expensive, but in that year, the first personal computer—the Altair 8800—was produced, which would change that forever. Just as the arrival of inexpensive computers from Commodore, Apple, and IBM led to a viable commercial game industry, they opened the door for a profitable educational software industry (see Figure 2.2).

At first, the emphasis in these products was far more on education than entertainment. They were little more than electronic versions of coursework with furry critters as teachers. In most cases, they were meant to supplement, not supplant, classroom curricula. But soon a new type of software appeared on the scene. It was called *edutainment software*.

Edutainment

Edutainment is a marriage of education and gameplay that can be experienced without supervision.

Figure 2.2
Math Blaster.

This marriage has always been a rocky one. Relationships need *balance* to sustain them. We'll come back to that word, *balance*, again and again in the following pages. One of the hardest jobs a game designer has is to balance the many elements of a game. But I'm getting ahead of myself.

EDUCATION VERSUS ENTERTAINMENT

The problem was that EDU came before TAINMENT. Education was emphasized so much that little more than lip service was paid to entertainment. This imbalance survives to this day. The dilemma is a tricky one. If the software fails to entertain, it can be even more boring than the worst lecturer. If the software concentrates too much on fun, it risks obscuring the learning objectives (see Figure 2.3). I will address this issue on later levels, but the secret to the balance here is pragmatic educators and game designers being willing to compromise, so that both have an opportunity to reach their goals.

The next wave of video games used for education was to drop the EDU entirely from Edutainment and bring the instructor back into the equation. These are commercial video games that may contain educational elements by their very nature but were not designed to be educational. One of my favorites, and one of the best computer games of all time, was Sid Meier's *Civilization* (see Figure 2.4).

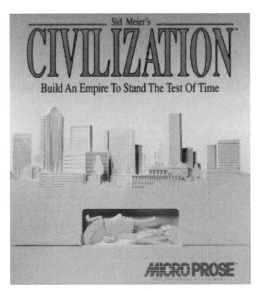

Figure 2.3
Introducing favorite characters doesn't help very much.

Figure 2.4
A commercial game that teaches.

My son Graham will tell you he learned some important history lessons from that game, including that dictatorships are a great system of government. You have nobody to answer to. You can do what you like. Until your people get so unhappy they revolt. Game over. Sorry, Graham.

Graham also learned strategy, tactics, diplomacy, arbitration, and leadership by running guilds in massively multiplayer games like *Everquest, Dark Age of Camelot,* and *World of Warcraft* starting at about age 10. In one early game, he told other players, many of whom were adults, that he was a cryogenics engineer from Seattle. In *Dark Age of Camelot,* he would be called upon to settle disputes between guilds run by people a lot older who prized his skills at arbitration.

And this brief anecdotal family history is supported by research. Constance Steinkuehler has done intriguing work on learning in massively multiplayer online games. James Paul Gee is another researcher in learning through video games. I commend the work of both and of their colleagues.

QUEST TO LEARN

Quest to Learn is an innovative school, currently teaching sixth and seventh graders but planning to eventually serve all middle and high school grades (see Figure 2.5). The year I entered academia, 2006, the initial design and development of Quest to Learn was being funded by a grant from the John D. and Catherine T. MacArthur Foundation. Collaborating with the Education Department of New York City, Quest to Learn focuses on digital literacy. The school first opened its doors in the fall of 2009, the same year I taught my first class as a game.

As their website explains, the school "immerses students in differentiated, challenge-based contexts, the school acknowledges design, collaboration, and systems thinking as key literacies of the 21st century." The school stresses that its approach is rigorous, not frivolous, and that students do not spend class time hunkered down in front of computer screens. Instead, classes are built around big ideas like "The Way Things Work." Then students are empowered to role-play within the class. For example, instead of teaching math, the school enables students to take on the role of mathematicians.

Figure 2.5
Quest to Learn.

I encourage you to look into Quest to Learn. These few paragraphs do not do the idea justice. It is a fascinating holistic approach to learning. You may well find ideas you can use. And on Level 16, I will share an idea at the Rochester Institute of Technology that is taking the multiplayer classroom to the next logical level beyond. Stay tuned.

This has been a brief history of how video games and video game design concepts have been used in education. But as you know, this book is not about using video games in the classroom. In fact, it's barely about using technology in the classroom. And it is also directed at teachers who do not have access to funds from large foundation grants. If nothing else, the multiplayer classroom will appeal to every miserly school system in the land. It uses the language and principles of video games to engage students with little to no out-of-pocket costs at all.

SECTION TWO

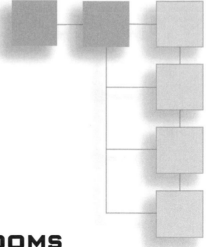

MULTIPLAYER CLASSROOMS

LEVEL 3

THEORY AND PRACTICE OF GAME DESIGN SYLLABI

Flashback: Summer of 2009

The first step in designing the new class was to decide what type of game to make it. With a total of 40 students possible in the class, multiplayer was an obvious choice, and the classroom is a real-time environment. There are real-time multiplayer versions of shooters and strategy games, as well as the multiplayer social games that have exploded in popularity on Facebook.

However, my preferred online gaming experience these days is persistent worlds, massively multiplayer online role-playing games or MMORPGs. Remember that first long acronym now shortened to MMOs? I've played many of these games, starting out with *Ultima Online* (1997) and continuing through *Lord of the Rings Online,* and the king of them all, *World of Warcraft*.

And while most of my commercial design work has been solo games, I've worked on MMOs from Cyan, Microsoft, and other companies, including a current project, *Star Trek: Infinite Space* for Gameforge. So the choice to design the class as a multiplayer role-playing game seemed like a natural one.

STAY FLEXIBLE

While multiplayer online games are played in real-time, they are designed first and played afterward. Even the inevitable gameplay updates for such issues as balancing and levels of difficulty, and the addition of new content, are all designed and tested in advance of implementation.

Thanks to the *Skeleton Chase* games, I'd also had experience with alternate reality games. Designing and running ARGs in real-time in the real world taught me that a level of flexibility and speed of implementation resembling improvisation worthy of Evelyn Salt, McGyver, or comedy troupes such as the *Dinner Detective* franchise, might be required.

In real life, stuff happens. Keep this in mind, if you intend to design your class as a game. As Robert Burns memorably reminded us in his poem "To a Mouse": "The best laid schemes o' Mice an' Men, gang aft agley." The best teachers think on their feet. But others may not want to venture into the wilderness that lies beyond the safety of the same notes, quips, and PowerPoints they've been leaning on for the past decade or more.

Having chosen the type of game I wanted to turn the class into, I next had a look at the syllabus I'd used in the fall of 2008. Here it is, as shown in Figure 3.1.

Pretty straightforward. Students rely on syllabi. While it may not be the contract some of them think it is, it should still give them their first detailed look at how they would be spending their time, and what would be expected of them.

CLASS OVERVIEW

After a brief description, I gave a broad overview of the class. The students would be divided into teams to write a game design proposal (also called a *concept document*) that in 30 pages would outline in some detail a game they would design as the class progressed. This would be their final project as well as a significant portion of their overall grade.

I listed the topics to be covered and laid out how many points each assignment would be worth on a 1,000-point scale. I matched that scale to the university's standard percentages for achieving the letter grades they would be awarded.

Indiana University, Bloomington
Department of Telecommunications

T367: Theory & Practice of Game Design

Section 27009
Fall 2008
Days and Times MW 1-2:15pm
Room 245 RTV Building

Instructor: Lee Sheldon
Office: Room 311 RTV Building
Phone: 855-6840
Office Hours: MW10:00-11:00am
Email: clsheldo@indiana.edu

Prerequisites: Three Previous Telecommunications Courses or Permission of Instructor

Description
From the earliest games played with sticks and pebbles through today's virtual worlds and ARGs, students will be exposed to game studies theory and video game design techniques, and will create proposals for games of their own.

Format
The underlying philosophy of this course is that the best learning is achieved by doing; so while there will be lectures and discussion on game theory and design issues and techniques, the emphasis will be on designing games.

Class time will be divided between lecture, workshop and review. At the beginning of the semester the emphasis will be on lectures and your reading. From the very beginning however we will be relating what we learn directly to the game designs. After selecting the games to be built, students will divide into teams (size of teams and number of designs determined by class size) to work on the designs.

Topics to be covered throughout the semester include:

- History of games
- Universal game design principles
- Video game development
- Video game research
- The video game industry
- Defining "game"
- Video game aesthetics
- Video game culture
- Player culture
- Narrative
- Serious games
- Video game design documents
- What we can borrow from passive media
- Non-linear structures
- Systemic gameplay & scripted gameplay
- ARGs (Alternate Reality Games)
- Discussion, review of the designs, post mortem

Grading Procedure

Grading is rigorous. The final grade will be based on a 1000 point scale as follows:

- Short papers analyzing elements of existing games (150 pts.)
- Quizzes (150 pts. total)
- Midterm Exam (250 pts.)
- Final Project: Video Game Proposal (300 pts.)
- Class attendance (75 pts.)
- Class participation (75 pts.)
- Extra credit for early completion of final proposal (10 pts./Monday; 5 pts./Tuesday; see calendar)
- Extra credit for text editing (25 pts.)

Spelling, grammar and punctuation must be proofed. Points will be deducted otherwise.

Grades and percentages:

A	93-100%	C	73-76%
A-	90-92%	C-	70-72%
B+	87-89%	D+	67-69%
B	83-86%	D	63-66%
B-	80-82%	D-	60-62%
C+	77-79%	F	0-59%

Attendance and Conduct

Attendance will be taken, and will count toward the final grade. You are expected to attend every class. Assignments are due at the *beginning* of every class. Late assignments will subtract from the grade for that assignment, one letter grade for each day the assignment is late.

Plagiarism, submitting assignments written by others, and other forms of academic misconduct are governed by university policy. In a word: DON'T.

Classroom conduct: Participate with civility and an abiding appreciation for the power of words. Respect others, even those who hold opposing views.

Required Text

Understanding Video Games. Egenfeldt-Nielsen et al.

Suggested Reading

Homo Ludens. Johan Huizinga.
Flow: The Psychology of Optimal Experience. Mihaly Csikszentmihalyi.
A Theory of Fun. Raph Koster.
Game Design (Second Edition). Bob Bates
Game Design: A Practical Approach. Paul Schuytema.
Rules of Play. Zimmerman & Salen.
The Art of Game Design: A Book of Lenses. Jesse Schell.
Character Development & Storytelling for Games. Lee Sheldon.

Figure 3.1
Fall 2008 syllabus.

The first three assignments in the list created the structure for the class and determined who would be placed on what team. All students were required to write a short pitch of a game they would like to make and then present it to the rest of the class. The class would then vote on their favorites. The top six vote getters would become the games for which the class created proposals. Students whose games did not win listed the top three games they would like to work on, and the roles they would like to play, again in order of preference.

The roles were chosen from the major team leads at a game development company.

- **Designer:** Usually the student whose idea had won.
- **Writer:** Responsible for organizing and editing the document as well as writing the story of the game.
- **Producer:** Responsible for arranging meeting times outside of class, seeing to it that the project progressed through the semester, and researching game development, budgets, and so on.
- **Tech Lead:** Responsible for the game's technical issues.
- **Art Lead:** Responsible for the images that would illustrate the document's text.
- **Marketing**: Responsible for working up a marketing plan, researching the competition, chances for success, and so on.

The students did not need to be proficient in any of these roles. If one of the students was an artist, fine. If not, they could find art on the Internet that most closely matched the style and substance of the game. The tech lead did not have to be a programmer, but rather would research game engines or decide if they would propose building one from scratch. In fact, all team members were encouraged to offer opinions and help in any other area. While they were each expected to write their section of the proposal, all were encouraged to read it in its entirety, both to offer suggestions and to help copy edit the text.

The syllabus concluded with a few lines about attendance and conduct. That was followed by the required text and a suggested reading list.

Multiplayer Classroom Syllabus

Now, let's have a look at the syllabus I wrote for the same class in the fall of 2009 (see Figure 3.2). The content in the course would remain the same. But this document would be the students' first detailed look at the multiplayer classroom.

To prepare them for what was to come, I stated simply, "This class is designed as a multiplayer game." But what could I adapt from the earlier syllabus, and what should remain the same? It was going to be a two-headed horse whatever I did, but I knew I wanted to grab students immediately with the game material.

First of all, the "Description" section of the class had no reason to change. It was the "Format and Grading Procedure" sections that would require the most thought.

I wanted to retain the listing of topics for discussion in the semester, but it wouldn't fit with the game jargon I would be using in the section, so I moved it to the end, right before the Reading List. Then I jettisoned everything else.

I still held back from descending entirely into gamer jargon. The word "monsters," for example, would more properly be "mobs." And I offered translations so they could see how the jargon would map to actions they would normally be expected to perform in class. While all students in the class had played video games, they had played a wide variety of types and not all students were hardcore gamers. Even so, as you can see from what follows, things began to change dramatically.

Taking quizzes and the midterm exam became "defeating monsters." Writing papers became "crafting." Class presentations where students presented the day's reading assignment became "quests."

All students were still required to do their reading homework, and five pop quizzes tested that they had done so. The class presentations took the place of my lectures on the reading. Depending upon the length of a reading selection, an individual student (solo quest), two students not in the same guild (pick-up group), or an entire guild would be responsible for presenting the material. As you'll see when we move to the next level in this book, this idea would need some massaging.

Indiana University, Bloomington
Department of Telecommunications

T367: Theory & Practice of Game Design
Section 29622
Fall 2009
Days and Times MW 1-2:15pm
Room 209 Ballantine Hall

Instructor: Lee Sheldon
Office: Room 311 RTV Building
Phone: 855-6840
Office Hours: MW 10:00-11:00 am
Email: clsheldo@indiana.edu

Prerequisites: Three Previous Telecommunications Courses or Permission of Instructor

Description
From the earliest games played with sticks and pebbles through today's virtual worlds and ARGs, students will be exposed to game studies theory and video game design techniques, and will create concept documents for games of their own.

Format
This class is designed as a multiplayer game.

Class time will be divided between fighting monsters (Quizzes, Exams etc.), completing quests (Presentations of Games, Research etc.) and crafting (Personal Game Premises, Game Analysis Papers, Video Game Concept Document etc.).

At the beginning of the semester everyone in the class will choose and name their avatars. The first task is to craft the premise of a game you would like to design. This may be a board game, video game (AAA, casual etc.), massively multiplayer game, alternate reality game, or...? Guilds to craft these games will be chosen, balanced as closely as possible by l33t skillz and interests. Guilds will choose their names. There will be five guilds of 5-6 members each depending upon final class size.

Grading Procedure
You will begin on the first day of class as a Level One avatar. Level Twelve is the highest level you can achieve:

Level	XP*	Letter Grade
Level Twelve	1860	A
Level Eleven	1800	A-
Level Ten	1740	B+
Level Nine	1660	B

Level Eight	1600	B-
Level Seven	1540	C+
Level Six	1460	C
Level Five	1400	C-
Level Four	1340	D+
Level Three	1260	D
Level Two	1200	D-
Level One	0	F

*Your level will be determined by experience points (XP) on a 2000 XP scale. You gain XP by defeating mobs, completing quests and crafting.

- Solo: Craft your own game proposal. (Written, 50 pts.)
- Solo: Present your game proposal to the class. (25 pts.)
- Solo: Sell your game proposal to the class. (**Extra credit**. 25 pts.)
- Raid: Guild reading presentation (75 pts. each person, 1 of these per guild)

- Pick-Up Group: 2-Player reading presentation (150 pts. each person, approx. 1 of 11 available, cannot team with fellow guild member) **OR**
- Solo: 1-Player reading presentation (150 pts. but easier than above, 1 of 2 available)

- Solo: Craft short report on *Senet* (Written, 75 pts.)
- Solo: Craft short analysis on board game of your choice (Written, 100 pts.)
- Solo: Craft analysis on video game of your choice (Written, 125 pts.)
- Solo: Defeat Five Random Mobs (5 written reading quizzes, 250 pts. total, 1 **extra credit** question per quiz)
- Solo: Defeat Level Boss (Midterm Exam, 400 pts.)
- Guild: Paper Prototype (50 pts. each)
- Guild: Craft Final Project: Video Game Proposal (Written, 400 pts.)
- Solo: Class attendance (300 skill pts. total, 10 to start. 290 additional pts. at 10 pts. per day of attendance)
- **Extra credit** for early completion of final proposal (10 pts./Monday; 5 pts./Tuesday; see calendar)
- Solo Camping: Text editing (**Extra credit**. 1 pt. per mistake. 50 pt. cap per player. First come first served. Each mob only spawns once.)
- Group: Peer Review Secret Ballot (**Extra credit**. 0-100 possible XP as follows:
    - Guild Leader 100 pts.
    - Raid Leader 75 pts.
    - Solid Guild Crafter 50 pts.
    - Needs Rez 25 pts.
    - Waste of Rations 0 pts.

Grading is rigorous. Spelling, grammar and punctuation must be proofed. Points will be deducted otherwise.

Attendance and Conduct
Attendance will be taken, and will count toward the final grade (see above). You are expected to attend every class. Assignments are due at the *beginning* of every class. Late assignments will subtract from the grade for that assignment, one letter grade for each day the assignment is late.

Plagiarism, submitting assignments written by others, and other forms of academic misconduct are governed by university policy. In a word: DON'T.

Classroom conduct: Participate with civility and an abiding appreciation for the power of words. Respect others, even those who hold opposing views.

Topics to be covered throughout the semester include:

- History of games
- Universal game design principles
- Video game development
- Video game research
- The video game industry
- Defining "game"
- Video game aesthetics
- Video game culture
- Player culture
- Narrative
- Serious games
- Video game design documents
- What we can borrow from passive media
- Non-linear structures
- Systemic gameplay & scripted gameplay
- ARGs (Alternate Reality Games)
- Discussion, review of the designs, post mortem

Required Text
Understanding Video Games. Egenfeldt-Nielsen et al.

Suggested Reading

Homo Ludens. Johan Huizinga.
Flow: The Psychology of Optimal Experience. Mihaly Csikszentmihalyi.
A Theory of Fun. Raph Koster.
Game Design (Second Edition). Bob Bates.
Game Design: A Practical Approach. Paul Schuytema.
Rules of Play. Zimmerman & Salen.
The Art of Game Design: A Book of Lenses. Jesse Schell.
Character Development & Storytelling for Games. Lee Sheldon.

Figure 3.2
Fall 2009 syllabus.

One game element not in the syllabus was a random factor. Many video games rely on a random factor to make certain the outcomes of player choices and actions are not always identical. A player may face mobs with identical statistics: equal strength, the same attack, and so on. Yet the amount of damage an attack might inflict is based on the computer version of dice rolls, just as it was with tabletop games like *Dungeons and Dragons*.

I brought dice to class and rolled them to determine which individual students and guilds would be responsible for the next class session's presentations. So one student might be hit by their solo quest and their guild quest on the same day. Another might not be chosen for either until very late in the semester.

This worried me. Students like everything spelled out. I printed out calendars of assignment due dates, the midterm, and when papers were due. They expected this. How would they react to fate taking a hand in their higher education? We shall see.

I let them know they would be choosing and naming their avatars. *Avatar* is another name for the character the player will direct throughout the game. James Cameron took the name of his blockbuster film from this game concept.

Avatar

An avatar is the online representation of a participant in a game or social network.

This was the first act they would perform in an MMO. I expected them to recognize exactly what was required of them. I also informed them in the syllabus that they would be separated into guilds.

Guild

A guild is a community in an online role-playing game. Guilds can be made up of any number of players, depending on the common goals and play style that guild members decide upon.

In the previous class, I had used the word *team* to describe a group of students who would work together to write the video game proposal that was the final project as before. Calling these teams *guilds* here was, like XP, an easy way to map game terminology onto existing class elements.

I kept the roles on each team the same, along with their responsibilities: designer, writer, producer, tech lead, art lead, and marketing. This was a missed opportunity I thought. I would try a more game-like naming of roles in another class. We'll see if that worked or not later on.

I gave the students too much latitude in choosing the type of game they wanted to design. I have learned the hard way that better work is done when the parameters of the assignment are much tighter. When the assignment is reduced to a specific problem, telling an architecture class to "draw blueprints for converting a factory into a luxury apartment building" is far more helpful than "draw blueprints for any building you like."

Such limits force more creativity from the students, and no matter how many times you warn them, when the sky's the limit, they will often try to do more than they possibly can accomplish.

GRADING PROCEDURE

The "Grading Procedure" section went through a radical overhaul. I knew that Experience Points (XP) were how players advanced in MMOs. Could I adapt the usual letter grades? In the table in the syllabus (refer to Figure 3.2), you'll see my first attempt. And while it looks good as a table, there are several flaws. The most obvious one is that in an MMO, we can set arbitrary amounts of XP necessary to advance.

The higher level the player, the more XP it takes to move from one level to the next. This is compensated for, in part, by greater amounts of XP awarded for tasks such as killing mobs. The only concern is that we find a balance between difficulty and reward.

The trouble with this chart was that they would have to earn 1200 points to reach Level 2, while it would only take another 660 points to reach the highest possible level. This is not only bad game design, but it's not very good class design either. Yet I blithely went ahead, assuming that they would understand this. They *could* see the exact amount of XP possible for any given task. Yet unless they did the math on their own, concentrating on the amount of XP they were awarded for a task as a percentage of the possible XP for that task, they would have no idea how they were doing.

Also, in an MMO, players traditionally level up much faster in the beginning than at the higher levels. So this particular XP system would not feel like a real

MMO. It would take me until the end of the semester to realize how much this worked against their immersion into the game. It would take me two more classes to begin to tackle the issue. Only in the current game is it beginning to finally feel right, but as we shall see on Level 9, something else needed to be added.

"Attendance and Conduct" came next, as before, with no changes. Next was the topic listing with no changes, the required textbook, and suggested reading.

I was ready, or so I thought, to put my idea to the test.

"Theory and Practice of Game Design" was a level 300 course with requirements that dictated most of the students would be upperclassmen. After the usual early semester juggling, we ended up with 30 students. I therefore divided the class into five guilds of six players each.

Here are the real-world terms in this chapter that map directly to game terms (see Table 3.1).

Table 3.1 Terminology Map

Student	Player
Teacher	Game Master
Student Name	Avatar Name
Team	Guild
Write	Craft
Take Quizzes/Exam	Defeat/Fight Monsters (Mobs)
Presentations	Quests
Individual Presentations	Solo Quests
Two or More Students Not in the Same Guild Presentations	Pick-up Group Quests
Lengthy Reading Assignment Presentations	Guild Quests
Real-World Abilities	l33t skillz

LEVEL 4

THEORY AND PRACTICE OF GAME DESIGN CLASS

Ballantine Hall is the tallest building on the Indiana University, Bloomington campus, and upon its completion in 1959, it was the largest academic building in the world. Because of its initial high cost, $6,242,422, air conditioning was not added to the building until 1977.

The geography of an MMO world involves several critical decisions. Designers can choose where a bridge crosses a river to funnel players to a particularly crucial location. We can design dungeons with dark, twisty passages to heighten the suspense of exploration, and to create nooks and crannies where nasty orcs can lurk, waiting to pounce on unwary adventurers. In the multiplayer classroom, however, we want to use the physical space we're given to its best advantage. It may seem like a limitation. It certainly can be a challenge. But the multiplayer class should not be designed to force huge changes in teachers' classrooms. It should instead encourage us to look at these spaces differently. How can they be used imaginatively, without time-consuming alteration?

Room 209 in Ballantine is an average-sized classroom with multimedia equipment and genuine blackboards. The most useful feature of Room 209, however, for the game designer looking to create a game world was its furniture. The student desks were chair desks: substantial metal chairs with l-shaped writing areas made of something vaguely resembling wood attached, as shown in Figure 4.1.

Figure 4.1
Ballantine Room 209.

ZONES

These desk chairs were perfect because of the need for something I've already mentioned flexibility. When the class was divided into guilds, the chairs could be rearranged into several "zones" separated by a few feet to divide the guilds. The zones, distinct areas within a game with their own ecosystems and challenges, were named after key words in game design.

Here are the zones:

- **Ocean of Immersion.** Immersion, or concentrating the attention on an activity such as a game, is an essential key to drawing the player into the world of the game.

- **Empathy Acres.** Empathy, the ability to figuratively put yourself in someone else's shoes, is important, if you want your players to feel emotion for the characters in a game.

- **Feedback Farms.** Players demand immediate feedback, the response a game returns to their input. This is why guns seem to work so much better in games than diplomacy.

- **Wandering Wastes.** *Wandering* is the term we use when a player loses direction in a game and does not know what to do next. This is bad.

- **Interface Island.** The interface between the game and the player should be intuitive and transparent. This serves to draw the player into the game world.

- **The Verbal Vale.** Game design, at its heart, is deciding what the player can do. This is indicated by active verbs: run, jump, talk, build, and so on.

Throughout the course of the semester, it was my plan to move the guilds from zone to zone. This meant that no guild would always be at the front or back of the class. My only idea in the first class was to break the common pattern of slackers with smart phones in their laps, texting instead of learning.

This worked well. At any given time, only two of the five guilds would be in the back of the classroom. Also, since the guilds were formed based on interest in a particular game idea and chosen roles, friends were split among the guilds, mixing those who weren't all that interested in participating with students eager to engage in discussion.

This came at a price. Up until this class, I had used a seating chart to teach myself the names of my students. The seating chart was useless because the guilds moved around the room every few weeks. It took me a lot longer than it had before to finally put names to faces.

Combat is a large part of the gameplay in many MMOs. Most of our game's combat took the form of PvE.

PvE: Player vs. Environment

PvE is gameplay where players fight against mobs controlled by programming we call *artificial intelligence* or AI.

In our case, PvE took the form of the quizzes and the midterm exam. Another example of flexibility these freestanding chair desks made possible was during PvP.

PvP: Player vs. Player

PvP is gameplay where players are pitted against one another.

PvP was introduced later in the semester, as we'll see. We rearranged the chair desks to create a space in the middle of the classroom where two guilds could face one another in two lines like opposing armies. The other guilds were arrayed in a circle around them like the walls of an arena.

On the first day of class, as planned, I greeted them with the statement that they all had F's. But I quickly segued into the explanation of how the class would be run as a multiplayer game. They were the players. I was the Game Master.

Game Master (GM)

A Game Master is in charge of the gameplay in a multiplayer game, organizing game sessions, enforcing rules, and arbitrating disputes. Sounds a lot like a teacher, doesn't it?

AVATARS

We went through the syllabus. Players were to think up avatar names for themselves; come up with a premise for a game they might like to design in class; and learn the rules to *Senet,* which I had posted online (see Figure 4.2). We would be playing and discussing this ancient Egyptian game, one of the earliest examples of a board game, during the following class session.

Figure 4.2
Senet, Egyptian game circa 3100 BC.

One week from that first day they introduced their avatars with pictures representing themselves. The portraits of the avatars could be drawn by the students or simply be images they had found online or elsewhere. It's worth noting that while a number of the players did not consider themselves hard-core gamers, or gamers at all, everyone understood the concept of an avatar.

Avatar Names

Bouren	Princess Peach
Walter	Neckface
DK	Thunder Cannon
Crunchy	Purple Haze
Panda.jpg	EPY
Spawn	Earthshaker
Sonya Blade	Floogin
Yoshi	Zombie Apocalypse
Laser Rocket Arm	Rookie
Kong	Domo
Damien	Castronaut
Anniesaur	Prinny
Coconut Monkey	Dr. Pheems
Sandsa	TBA
Dr. Love	Jake the Barbarian

A word on consistency in game design. Unless they are creating a world where anachronisms are specifically acceptable, game designers should strive for consistency in theme, story, events, characters, artwork, music, and so on. A consistent world is a world that encourages the player's willing suspension of disbelief and smoothes the path to immersion in the game experience.

In a classroom, though, as in MMOs, the designer must deal with human beings wanting to make their individual stamp on the world, especially with their avatars. Everyone has her or his own ideas about what is creative or funny. So, for example, as much as a designer may strive to create a world that is true to a medieval fantasy setting, players may (and do) name their avatars just about anything. Like their choices or not, these are their choices. It provides them with a sense of ownership and gives them a stake in the game, even as it may drive more consistency-minded, aesthetically aware designers, teachers, and players up the wall. Other than the usual list of offensive words, let them do it. Don't fight it. Embrace it! Somebody who wants to name her avatar Zombie Apocalypse should have that privilege.

Players took turns pitching their game premises to the class. Everyone then voted on which premises they liked the best. The highest five vote-getters became the games they would design.

I asked players to list their choices for which game they would like to work on in order of preference and to list what roles they would like to play. Listed in Table 4.1 are the guild names they chose and the titles of the games they would be designing.

And we were off. First, playing *Senet*; then crafting an analysis of its gameplay. Random dice rolls determined who would be responsible for the next class sessions' quests. Much to my surprise, the students not only did not mind this element of chance, but they accepted it. More than that, they seemed to enjoy it, commenting on the dice rolls as they would the tricks chance played on them in games.

The first reading quizzes in the guise of surprise attacks by mobs wiped almost the entire player base.

Table 4.1 Guilds and Games

Guilds	Games
Slug Machine	*Bullet Wounds*
Apocalypse Later	*City State*
Anytime Football	*Touchdown Dice*
The Church of Fonz	*Solar Race*
The Shogunate	*5 Rings*
Magma	*Volcano*

Figure 4.3
Many a raid has wiped courtesy of *World of Warcraft's* Lich King.

WIPE

A wipe is a disastrous encounter in either PvE or PvP where all the members of a party of adventurers are wiped out by their opponents. The results resemble Figure 4.3.

I mentioned learning from your mistakes in the introduction. Here is an obvious example. Up until the first random mob attack, reading quizzes were a weather report that might or might not come true. They depended upon the sometimes shaky presentations with my occasional interjections and clarifications. After most of the class wiped, many immediately started reading, and then challenging the presenters. Many, but not all.

As I've said, I haven't been teaching very long. Yet even in my limited experience, I've come to realize that not every student can be reached. It's a sobering, saddening fact. There were still a few students in this first iteration of the multiplayer classroom who, while they seemed to enjoy the time they spent in class, and even occasionally participated vigorously in discussions of specific video games they'd played, missed too many classes and studied too little.

They were like players encountered in any MMO, wearing armor too fragile and wielding weapons too blunted, to survive.

Peer Review

Since these players were scattered among the six guilds, and a large amount of XP would be awarded both for the final game proposal and guild presentations, they may have assumed they would get a free ride on the backs of their guild mates. They seem to have missed that part of the syllabus called *Peer Review*. It has been in all of my syllabi before and after implementation of the multiplayer classroom. I'll repeat the version for this class. As indicated in the syllabus, the XP awarded would be on the following scale.

Peer Review Secret Ballot

1. Guild Leader: 100 pts.

2. Raid Leader: 75 pts.

3. Solid Guild Crafter: 50 pts.

4. Needs Rez: 25 pts.

5. Waste of Rations: 0 pts.

"Waste of Rations" was a wonderfully derogatory term I learned from my first manager in the games industry, François Robillard, a former captain in the Canadian army. As good as it was in describing someone who contributed nothing, I'd missed a better description. I would rectify that in the next class I taught.

Guild members ranked their fellow member's efforts. I was concerned about two potential issues with this: First, all guild members might simply agree to give each other the full 100 XP. Second, a guild member with a gripe against another might grade that person down simply to get at them.

Here was another case, like random dice rolls, where I was surprised. In no guilds in the class did everyone earn 100 pts. It was clear from participation and ability that the 100s were earned by those who received them. And when members were reviewed far lower, including one student who simply vanished a few weeks into the semester, it was clear they deserved the evaluation.

These low-performing students, every one of them, failed to take advantage of any of the other extra credit opportunities available, including the easiest one of all: farming (see Figure 4.4).

Figure 4.4
Farming as a profession in China.

FARMING

Farming is killing the same mobs—usually a much lower level than the player—over and over again as the most efficient way to gain levels and loot.

We used as our textbook *Understanding Video Games* by Simon Egenfeldt-Nielsen, Jonas Heide Smith, and Susana Pajares Tosca. It had been published just the year before, and I chose it because it was the only book I could find that combined game development and game studies in one place and was easy enough to understand for beginning students.

The problem with it was that it was apparently never copy edited, nor edited by anyone who knows anything about games. There were dozens of errors from simple typos to errors of fact, such as placing *Doom*'s release in the wrong decade. Our class farmed over 80 such errors for extra credit. Of course, those who found the most needed the extra XP the least.

As the semester progressed, I noticed a big mistake I had made in my quest system. The novelty of the students handling the lectures only went so far—particularly when too many players were turning out to be no better than the most boring of teachers, presenting black bulleted points on white backgrounds; doing no more than reading them aloud.

I managed to light a fire under some of the later presenters by encouraging the use of other resources like YouTube, but it would have been wiser to have given them up-front examples of especially inventive presentations. TED talks are a great resource! And for my current class, I've divided the grade into two parts: clarity of the presentation and the inventiveness of its delivery.

Other than calling the midterm exam a *Boss Mob*, the most powerful mob in a level or dungeon, it was an ordinary exam. But I tried something different with reading quizzes later in the semester.

I'd always had an extra credit final question on the reading quizzes. For the last two quizzes, I added six more extra credit questions that players could earn in PvP Guild vs. Guild combat. I didn't change the seating for these two events. I wanted something similar to the buzzer game show contestants hit on TV, but I had no technology. So I settled on giving each guild their own word to shout out, if they wanted to take a shot at the answer. The words were: laugh, groan, yell, cough, burp, and cry.

Anyone on a guild could provide the answer, whether they shouted first or not. So, after a brief consultation among themselves, the guilds could collaboratively come up with the answer. This worked well. Everybody had a good time. Trash-talking between guilds was inspired. And everyone had a chance to share in the fiero.

Trash Talking

Trash talking is boastful, taunting chat, at times laced with l33t speak and profanity, that is meant to assert authority before, during, or after a contest.

l33t Speak

l33t speak is a pseudo-language that began on bulletin boards in the 1980s, often simply a product of misspellings; then it prospered as a means to get around language filters in multiplayer gaming and social networks. Elements of l33t speak are now in general usage, particularly in texting and tweeting. Examples include "c" instead of "see," "u" instead of "you," "teh" instead of "the," "pwned" instead of "owned." Replacing vowels with numbers and characters is also common as in "l33t" itself, derived from "elite."

The success of these two events was to give me an idea for a new, much more gamelike, approach to preparing for the midterm.

Prototypes were created for the games that students were designing. Rules were put online a week before they were to be played by the other guilds (see Figure 4.5).

No MMO is made up of a single game mechanic where players are only required to do one thing to achieve a single result. There are many different types of mini-games built into them. There were mini-games in this class as well. Students played *Senet*, their own game prototypes, PvP as I've just described, and a final PvP tournament we'll get to shortly. I learned to write scripts by watching TV and movies. I learned to write and design video games by playing them. Ample opportunity to play a variety of games was a cornerstone of the MC, just as it is in an MMO.

After the prototypes were played and analyzed, it was time to pitch their ideas to publishers. These publishers were role-played in this class by two fellow faculty members, Edward Castronova and Norbet Herber, both familiar with video game design and the gaming industry. They listened to the pitches and then in character critiqued them. This was a good idea of what the students might expect should they decide to pursue careers in the commercial video game industry. I've tried to do this with every class I teach where students have a final project. When I teach screenwriting, I bring in actors to read selected scenes aloud. Doses of the real world can be inspiring and encouraging. If they scare off someone who is uncertain if they've found their dream career path, it's better to do it now than later.

At last, the final proposals were due and XP rewarded. Another way that the classroom experience mapped directly to games occurred when there were a number of graded assignments along the way. Video games would be incredibly boring and discouraging if the only reward came after defeating the boss mob on the final level. Incremental rewards are terribly important for keeping players engaged.

One final point: Games "grade" a player's performance by attrition. While you could lose XP and even a level in some early MMOs like *Everquest*, today a player is always gaining XP when he is victorious. This way of looking at achievement has something to teach us educators. Letter grades—the way we align them as penalties for failure—and how our educational system focuses on achievement learning can hinder student progress; the direct opposite of experience points mounting to the stars. We will explore this important difference later on.

Anytime Football

Set-Up
- Give 5 cards to each player
- Place the remaining stack on the draw pile.

Game Play
- Flip a coin to see who starts on offense.
- Place the marker at the 20 yard line of the side the defense chooses.
- Each play both players choose a card from their hand to play. The cards are special "power ups" for different positions and different plays. It is written on the card what the advantage will be when matched with the opposing card.
- Offense then chooses pass or run.
- Then starts a series of dice battling, offense rolls first. Roll all 5 dice at once, keep which dice you want to build on. Then roll again choose the dice again. Then Roll a third time, after the third roll, you dice are fixed.
- Defense then rolls in the exact same sequence
- If the offense wins the roll the outcome is as follows (do not move yet)-
    - Run
        - 3 of a kind—5 yards
        - Full House—10 yards
        - Four card straight—15 yards
        - Four of a kind—20 yards
        - Five card straight—25 yards
        - Five of a kind—touchdown
- If you choose to pass the yardages double.
- If the defense wins the roll the yardages become negative (sack). If the defense wins with a five card straight, it is a sack for a loss of 25 yards. If the defense rolls a five of a kind it is an interception for a touchdown. If the defense rolls 5 aces, the opponents quarterback is injured for the rest of the game and passing yards are cut in half.
- Before the offense moves, you must apply the outcome of the card play as well. (directions on the cards)
- Down and distance is consistent with real football.
- On fourth down the offense may choose to punt or kick a field goal. No cards are used for kicking.

- Punt
- Each player rolls one Die simultaneously 5 Times.
- If the offense wins—
    - All 5 rolls—offense receives a first down via roughing the kicker.
    - 4 rolls— offense places the ball wherever they like for the opponent to take over.
    - 3 rolls—offense punts the ball 40 yards.
    - 2 rolls—offense punts the ball 30 yards
    - 1 roll—offense punts the ball 20 yards.
    - 0 rolls—defense blocks the punt and takes the ball at the line of scrimmage.
- Field Goal
- Battle roll just like a punt
- The max field goal is 60 yards
- If the offense wins—
    - All 5 rolls—FG made from 60 yards or less.
    - 4 rolls—FG made from 50 yards or less.
    - 3 rolls—FG made from 40 yards or less.
    - 2 rolls—FG made from 30 yards or less.
    - 1 roll—FG made from 20 yards or less.
    - 0 rolls—Defense blocks the kick and takes over on offense from the original line of scrimmage.

Winning
- 7 points are awarded for touchdowns.
- 3 points are awarded for field goals.
- First player to reach 35 points first wins the game.

Figure 4.5
Anytime Football's rules for *Touchdown Dice*.

Here are the real-world terms in this chapter that map directly to game terms (see Table 4.2).

Table 4.2 Terminology Map	
Section of the Classroom	Zone
Quizzes/Midterm	PvE
Student Competitions	PvP
Teacher	Game Master
Entire Class Does Badly on a Quiz	Wipe
Take Quizzes/Exam	Defeat/Fight Monsters (Mobs)
Copy Editing	Farming
Midterm Exam	Boss Mob
Incremental Grades	Rewards

Time now to have a look at the second iteration of the multiplayer classroom where mistakes made in this class led to a few lessons learned, although some issues continued to annoy. Appropriately enough the class I taught in the spring of 2010 was called Multiplayer Game Design. And take a look at Table 4.2 for a comparison of real-world terms and game terminology.

STUDENT EVALUATION QUOTES

Indiana University, as with most institutions of higher learning, uses student evaluations as part of the process to determine how teachers are doing in class, or what students thought about the learning environment of class. While I always spent the last day of a class soliciting opinions and advice for the future from students, here is a sampling of quotes from their official evaluation sheets.

"The learning environment for this course was really fun and entertaining. The instructor could improve the course by making some of the games more fair when deciding on points."

"Fun. Educational. Learning through experience. [We should have played] some video games in class to better show examples."

"Our big assignments should have their *requirements discussed/described.*"

"Fun and light-hearted. Could have been more structured. We kind of made it up as we went."

"Didn't like the textbook. It was almost as bad as my writing."

"It was a relaxed, fun environment. I enjoyed the "guild" setup as it really made me feel comfortable and sociable. The lingo used in the course made me feel that at least I was among fellow gamers. I feel like we could have benefitted with less student presentations and more teacher instruction. There's only so much I can learn from a PowerPoint. Mr. Sheldon has a lot of experience, and I'd like to learn from that more directly."

"It was a good idea to treat this class like a game, but the mechanics need to be worked on. I liked having a guild to work with."

"Very laid-back and jovial. A very fun group to exchange ideas and debate. Celebrates the subject. Lock down the rules on grading. Quite a few times I was surprised or unsure of how we would be graded."

"The class was full of people interested in video games, which made the class a great learning environment. More explanation on assignments."

"I like the video game feel of the class. Forming the guilds and working within them to complete tasks (i.e., debates, quizzes, etc.) was fun. I learned a lot more about video games now than before. The environment just made some of the dry material (i.e., edutainment section and other learning theories) more fun. I would give more detail on the prototype design documents. I wanted to know more about what you liked/disliked, more suggestions, etc., to make the final concept document better."

"Very experimental and collaborative."

"Very encouraging for discourse. Further integrate the gaming idea into the class [would have been helpful]—(i.e., intertwine elements of class-work with gaming)."

Case Histories

Introduction

Just over a year has passed since Jesse Schell's talk that began the interest in the multiplayer classroom that has resulted in this book. Yet already participants in the Gaming the Classroom forums, and I assume elsewhere, are trying this new form of teaching in their own classrooms. I asked those on the forums who were designing their classes as games, if they would contribute short case histories of their experiences.

These case histories are scattered throughout the remainder of the book. Some are simply stories, while others are more formal articles. In addition to anecdotal evidence, you will occasionally find both quantitative and qualitative results. Lengths may vary, approaches may vary, but each adds insights that would be missing had I not included them. All share two things in common: an abiding interest in achieving the finest education we can provide for our children and a curiosity about coursework designed as games.

The first article follows immediately. The rest are distributed throughout the book to give you an occasional oasis of relief from the desert of my prose.

One of the first objections raised to my idea of a multiplayer classroom was that it might work fine for a game design class, but it probably wouldn't work in other courses. These case histories should go a long way toward answering that concern. Fields of study are History, Math, Biology, Computer Science, Media, and Education.

You'll find courses taught at universities or community colleges, high schools, and one from a middle school. They are from all over the United States.

Here in their own words are these educators' adventures in designing coursework as a game.

Case History 1

Marked Tree High School

Denishia Buchanan

Biology Teacher

Marked Tree High School

Marked Tree, Arkansas

Our first case history comes from Denishia Buchanan, a biology teacher in Arkansas (see Figure CH1.1). She notes that 80% of her students fall below the poverty line and typically do not perform well in school, with many failing to graduate.

An avid gamer, Denishia was a natural when it came to designing a multiplayer classroom. Her leveling system adds an ingenious time element, and her quests are given by special quest givers within the classroom, such as the one who consented to pose with her below in Figure CH1.1.

Her questing system is so successful—have a look at the remarkable statistics— that she's planning quests for her Anatomy class. And the school's administrators are encouraging other teachers to do the same.

Here is her own quest to reach and teach students more used to struggling than success.

Figure CH1.1
Denishia Buchanan with one of her quest givers: Princess Sodabottle.

INTRODUCTION

Gaming and education aren't usually two words that go together; however, after reading an article published by *The Chronicle of Higher Education* detailing Lee Sheldon's unique technique of creating a gaming experience for his multiplayer design class, I was intrigued. If pop culture has taught us anything, it's that most teenagers would rather spend more time playing video games than finishing school work. The article explained that Mr. Sheldon uses experience points in his class instead of the traditional point system that is used in modern education. His entire classroom is based on popular gaming themes. His classwork is set up like quests that may either be solo'd or completed in a pick-up group, as well as having groups of students sit together to form guilds.

Upon reading the article, I began brainstorming on my own version of gaming in the classroom. Being an avid gamer for the majority of my life allowed me to use my personal experiences in various gaming situations to design a high school version of Mr. Sheldon's technique. Beginning in the 2010–2011 school year, three sophomore level biology classes began playing "Biology Quest."

Students who play "Biology Quest" are required to reach levels of achievement in a certain amount of time. To reach these levels, students must gather experience points (XP). Students have various opportunities to obtain these points. For example, Level 1 requires 100 XP and has a due date of one week. Students are required to quest (complete various assignments) to gain these 100 experience points. When the due date arrives, whatever the student has gathered goes into the grade book. For example, Amanda has completed all three section reviews for Chapter 1 worth 10 XP and made a 60 on the Chapter 1 exam. A 70% is recorded for Amanda's Level 1 score. As the level requirements increase, students must complete more assignments to achieve at higher levels.

In addition to questing experience, students are also awarded "Biology Bucks." Each quest is given a monetary value based upon how difficult and what level the quest is. Students use the Biology Bucks to buy classroom supplies and even hall passes to the library or restroom.

"Biology Quest" is a way for students to immerse themselves into the discipline. It allows students to expand their knowledge further than a typical classroom would allow. Students are given the freedom to pick and choose assignments that they feel they would perform best at. In "Biology Quest," every learning style has the opportunity to shine.

LEVELS

Level	Experience Points Required	Time to Complete	Semester
1	100	1 week	Fall
2	200	2 weeks	Fall
3	400	2 weeks	Fall
4	800	4 weeks	Fall
5	1600	4 weeks	Fall
6	3200	6 weeks	Spring
7	6400	6 weeks	Spring
8	12800	6 weeks	Spring

For the fall semester

A	2760 points
B	2480 points
C	2449 points
D	1872 points
F	Below 2182

For the spring semester

A	21696 points
B	19296 points
C	16896 points
D	14496 points
F	Below 14495

QUESTING

Quests are class assignments that students complete for experience points and Biology Bucks. Quests are assigned experience points based upon how difficult the quest is to complete. In "Biology Quest," students are only allowed to complete quests solo. They may help one another, but copying is strictly prohibited.

Quests are provided to students by "quest givers." These are different inanimate and living objects throughout the room that provide quests to the students. The quest-givers are Big Chief Waterwalker, our classroom mascot; Luke and Waylon, the classroom turtles; Oscar the Vile, our very hungry cichlid; and Princess Sodabottle, our recycled plastic skeleton model. Each "quest giver" presents quests to students in a narrative. The narrative explains what is expected on the quest, as well as what rewards will be provided. For example, see the following note.

It's All in the Strategy

Hey man. . . .Waylon just won't listen to me. I've been trying to tell him about k-strategists and r-strategists. He just doesn't listen. This is what I want you to do. I want you to write a children's book about k and r strategists. Explain it in terms that Waylon could understand. After all, he is only three years old. Make the book at least six pages long. Be sure to include pictures of the different kind of strategists. Waylon always judges a book by its cover, so make the cover SUPER exciting!

50 XP and 5 Bucks

Quests are provided for the students in two forms. One, all quests are placed in a classroom quest log booklet. This booklet contains quests from every quest giver from Level 1 to the current level that students are completing. Second, at the beginning of a new level, all students receive a copy of each quest to put in their own quest log folder. This ensures that all students know what quests are available for the current level.

Quests are designed to reach every skill level and learning style. Each level has quests that appeal to visual learners, auditory learners, and kinesthetic learners. Students complete a survey to determine their learning style. They are then challenged to develop skills in learning styles other than the style they were most competent in.

Quests are designed to expand student thinking. Although some quests are small review sections or worksheets, the majority of quests are high-level assignments. Students must create websites, make brochures, write essays, create learning cubes, make models, develop analogies, write rap songs, and several different multimedia projects.

For 25 minutes each day, I teach students the "lore" of biology. This is usually presented as a whole group classroom activity, lecture, or a lab activity. During this time, I present the essential information about the current topic of study. Quests will provide more detailed "lore" through an inquiry process. After this is completed, the students have 20 minutes to quest.

During quest time, students have access to computers. They may use these computers to access the Internet or use programs such as Windows Movie Maker to complete their quests. Students also have access to an extensive craft supply. They may use boxes, Styrofoam balls, clay, markers, colored pencils, and so on, to complete their quests. Students may also leave the classroom to do library research. Students must use every minute of quest time on quests. They aren't allowed to sit and look pretty.

Quests must be turned in complete and perfect. If the quest giver requires a project to be colorful and the student turns in the work uncolored, no points will be received. The student must finish the project. If the quest is a worksheet, lab, or bookwork, all questions must be answered to the fullest extent. All essays turned in must follow the English department's guidelines for sentence structure, paragraph structure, and essay format. If a student fails a dungeon quest (tests), then the dungeon must be attempted again until they receive a 60%.

REWARD SYSTEM

Students are rewarded for completing quests not only in quest XP, but also in Biology Bucks. Biology Bucks are dollars that students can spend within the Biology classroom. In student's quest logs, each quest denotes the XP value, as well as a monetary value. Most quests award $1–$20 Biology Bucks, depending on the difficulty and the time required to complete a project. When the quest has been graded and deemed worthy, students will receive the quest back, as well as the Biology Bucks at which the quest was valued. If a student has completed a quest above and beyond the required elements, then extra money is allotted, and the quest gets placed on a wall of fame.

Students may use their Biology Bucks in several ways. First, they may use it at various vendors to buy needed classroom supplies, such as pencils and paper. Secondly, they may use the money to obtain special hall passes, such as bathroom or library passes. Finally, they may use their money at the Auction House.

I provide the students with two vendors for classroom supplies. The first vendor sells students classroom supplies. They may buy one pencil for one Biology Buck. The same is true for paper. A spiral notebook will cost the student $3 Biology Bucks. A paper folder will only cost $1. Other items may be rented from the second vendor. Rentable items include Biology Books or Classroom Reference Books. These are rented with a $5 dollar deposit. When the book is returned, the $5 Biology Bucks are returned.

Every nine weeks, students are invited to attend an auction. Auctions are funded by the Science Club through various fundraisers. Auctions are presented to students in two ways: a silent auction and a typical English auction. The silent auction involves big-ticket items that every single questing class can participate in. For instance, in this nine-week period, students are bidding on a $100 Visa gift card. Students must place their bid for the gift card in a box. After the auction expires, the highest bidder wins the card. The English auction pits students in the same class period in bidding wars vying for various items, including hall passes, coupon books, small gift certificates, lotions and sprays, as well as food items.

STUDENT OPINIONS

My students are very pleased with this form of class. Students have expressed that knowing exactly how many points are expected of them and offering various methods of obtaining these points allow them to achieve higher. Several other students said that having a reward at the end of nine weeks (like our auctions) was great motivation for them to do more work. Students state that they would like other teachers to use this method in their classrooms.

The classes that are not questing complain that it is unfair and that if they had that opportunity when they were in Biology, they would have scored much higher. My AP Biology class begs me to begin questing with them. Several students have come up to me in the hallway and said that they cannot wait to be in my class so that they can quest.

Because of questing, many students feel more confident in science. A lot of students have told me that they would like to pursue a career in nursing, veterinary medicine, nuclear medicine, and engineering, just to name a few. Students feel that when they are given a choice in the type of work they do in classes, they will produce more work with more effort.

DATA ANALYSIS

Marked Tree High School is 80% free and reduced lunch, meaning that 80% of our students fall below the poverty line. Typically, these students do not perform well in school, and many of them fall short of high school graduation. Many students that do make it to graduation do not go on to college. Most never even take their ACT.

In December of 2009, 62% of the sophomores taking Biology were passing with a D or higher. These students were taking a Biology class taught in the traditional format. In December 2010, 98% of sophomores taking Biology were passing with a D or higher, 36% of whom had an A or a B. This is compared to 2009's 10% having an A or a B. The increase in scores is in direct relation to questing.

Each quarter, students must take an End of Course Practice Test. Students must score 60% to be considered proficient in Biology. The EoC is a comprehensive test. In October 2009, students were 29% proficient or higher on this exam. In the 2010 administration, 68% were proficient or advanced. At this time, the 2010 students had been questing for nine weeks. The second administration was given in December. In 2009, students scored 31% proficient or advanced. The results from the 2010 test showed that 81% of the students were scoring proficient or advanced.

Not only is questing increasing the percentage of students scoring proficient or advanced, but it is also increasing the number of students that are advanced in Biology. In 2009, only 3% of the students were scoring advanced. This year, 55% are scoring advanced.

Conclusion

Questing, without a doubt, increases student motivation, student attitude, and student performance. Data proves this fact. Students in my classroom are doing three times the amount of work that students completed in previous years, and they are doing it with joy and without complaint. Work that is turned in shows that the student has spent time and energy on it. All work shows that the student took pride in completing this work. Allowing students to choose assignments that they feel they are good at provides an atmosphere for students to extend their thinking and dive deeper into a topic than ever before.

Questing has provided an opportunity for my students that they never had before. Through questing, they feel confident in their work. Knowing that they can succeed in a difficult class makes them want to pursue more opportunities within that subject. I have several students who would never have considered taking AP Biology before, and now they have signed up for the class.

My students have asked me to extend questing into other classes. I will do this. I have already begun planning questing assignments for the second semester of my Anatomy class. My administration is seeing our students' performance increase by leaps and bounds and because of this is encouraging other core subjects to incorporate this type of learning into their classroom.

LEVEL 5

MULTIPLAYER GAME DESIGN SYLLABI

As with "Theory and Practice of Game Design," I had taught "Multiplayer Game Design" before. In the spring of 2008, it was a regular lecture, workshop, and review class. Instead of a combination of practical game design and video game studies course, this class was, as I say in the syllabus that follows, intended to introduce students to the "design elements and production requirements necessary to create and maintain online games." In short, it involved far more practical application than theory.

You will also notice that while the syllabus makes it sound as if the entire class would work on one virtual world project, in fact, I divided the 31 students in the class into teams to produce five concept documents. As noted previously, concept documents are the same as game proposals. In our case, these were 30-page, double-spaced documents describing all aspects of the game ideas from story and gameplay through budget and marketing.

Virtual World

A virtual world is a digital world that may or may not be a game. *Second Life,* for example, is not a game, even though many can experience it simultaneously, and it contains games. It is more of a social networking space. Virtual worlds are often *persistent* worlds, meaning that time passes within the world even when a person's avatar may not be present. MMOs are persistent worlds.

As our primary text, I chose Richard Bartle's *Designing Virtual Worlds*, still the best introduction to virtual world history and production. If you have an interest in attempting to create one of these, read this book.

THE 2008 SYLLABUS

I prepared the syllabus shown in Figure 5.1 for the Spring 2008 version of "Multiplayer Game Design."

One thing to notice about this earlier syllabus and the one on Level 3 is that there are far fewer tasks that contribute to the final grade. A difference between traditional methods of teaching and the multiplayer classroom is that there are many more grades in an MC (multiplayer classroom). Yet, this is precisely what the students expect. In an MMO, there is an unlimited supply of repeatable tasks to guarantee that players can always level up. In an MC, there must be enough assignments to replicate that aspect of gameplay (many opportunities for XP) and rewards (many opportunities for incremental rewards).

GRADING AND ATTENDANCE

I have a student friend in law school who has a class where the entire grade is the final exam. This makes some sense. If an attorney wants to practice law in a particular state (or group of states with a reciprocal agreement), the attorney must pass a single bar exam. It's all or nothing. This would seem logical in the multiplayer classroom because we've already looked at boss raids where players fail multiple times before they figure out the precise tactics and strategy to defeat the boss mob. The difference is that those players have spent weeks achieving smaller victories, which are also rewarded on a smaller scale.

In a traditional grading system, if you miss an assignment, you lose points. In the MC, you can always make up the assignment—you simply earn less XP. In my earlier classes, perfect attendance is rewarded with 100 pts. Students who miss classes have points deducted from that total. In the MC, students are awarded XP for every class they attend.

This may sound like the same thing, and in mathematical terms, it is. However, the feeling for the students is different, and this feeling of attrition instead of subtraction is familiar to them from games. They are more comfortable with it. They know how to game this system: Show up and gain XP. It's easy!

Indiana University, Bloomington
Department of Telecommunications

T366: Multiplayer Game Design

Section 25059
Spring 2008
Days and Times MW 4-5:15pm
Room 226 RTV Building
Prerequisites: Permission of Instructor

Instructor: Lee Sheldon
Office: Room 311 RTV Building
Phone: 855-6840
Office Hours: MW1:00-2:00pm
Email: clsheldo@indiana.edu

Description
Focus is on massively-multiplayer online games and virtual worlds. Students will be introduced to the design elements and production requirements necessary to create and maintain online games. We will study various existing worlds e.g. *World of Warcraft*, *Lord of the Rings Online*, *Second Life* and *A Tale in the Desert* (list of worlds studied is subject to change); and then lay the groundwork for creating new ones. Students will be required to do hands-on work for one of the new virtual worlds being developed in the Department of Telecommunications.

Format
The underlying philosophy of this course is that the best learning is achieved by doing; so while there will be lectures and discussion on multiplayer game design issues and techniques, the emphasis will be on building them.

Class time will be divided between lecture, workshop and review. At the beginning of the semester the emphasis will be on lectures and your reading. From the very beginning however we will be relating what we learn directly to the virtual world project. Students will divide into teams to work on various sections of world design e.g. management, design, art, geography, lore, engines, systems, customer service etc.

Topics to be covered throughout the semester include:

- Introduction, forming the development team, project management
- Building a blueprint of the game: the design documents
- The history of MUDs and virtual worlds
- What we can borrow from passive media
- Theme, style, genre, characters, story
- Non-linear structures
- Scope & scale, dynamic content
- Other human beings, player types
- Social interaction: communication, guilds, politics, factions
- Systemic gameplay & scripted gameplay

- Maintaining the world, content delivery, customer service
- Game/Entertainment Industry and where virtual worlds fit
- Discussion, review of the design, post mortem

Grading Procedure
Grading is rigorous, based on:
- Short papers analyzing elements of existing virtual worlds (200 pts)
- Quizzes (150 pts total)
- Concept Document (400 pts)
- Class participation (150 pts)
- Attendance (100 pts)

Spelling, grammar and punctuation must be proofed. Points will be deducted otherwise.

Grades and percentages:

A	93-100%	C	73-76%
A-	90-92%	C-	70-72%
B+	87-89%	D+	67-69%
B	83-86%	D	63-66%
B-	80-82%	D-	60-62%
C+	77-79%	F	0-59%

Attendance and Conduct
Attendance will be taken, and will count toward the final grade. You are expected to attend every class. Assignments are due at the *beginning* of every class. Late assignments will subtract from the grade for that assignment, one letter grade for each day the assignment is late.

Plagiarism, submitting assignments written by others, and other forms of academic misconduct are governed by university policy. In a word: DON'T.

Classroom conduct: Participate with civility and an abiding appreciation for the power of words. Respect others, even those who hold opposing views.

Required Text
Designing Virtual Worlds. Richard Bartle.
Character Development and Storytelling for Games. Lee Sheldon.

Suggested Reading
Developing Online Games. Mulligan and Petrovsky.
Massively Multiplayer Game Development. Thor Alexander et al.
Synthetic Worlds. Edward Castronova.
Community Building on the Web. Amy Jo Kim
My Tiny Life: Crime and Passion in a Virtual World. Julian Dibbell
A Theory of Fun. Raph Koster
Flow: The Psychology of Optimal Experience. Mihaly Csikszentmihalyi.

Figure 5.1

Spring 2008 syllabus.

Experience has borne out the benefit of this subtle change. Last semester's class, "Introduction to Game Design," had nearly perfect attendance: Three absences that were unexcused, but I was informed of them in advance, one excused absence, and only one where a student failed to show up, although he apologized after the fact. I will reproduce attendance sheets for all four classes later in the book.

It wasn't until the class I'm currently teaching that I finally introduced a system of leveling that actually *began* at least to solve the problems of students leveling too slowly at the beginning and being uncertain how they were progressing. It's no coincidence that it is much simpler with multiple graded tasks.

More work for the teacher? Obviously. More *grading*? Ick! However, the workload is balanced by the fact that individual lessons are not prepared by the teacher to present to students. They do the preparation. The teacher is the Game Master. All you need to do is sit back and moderate their teaching. If they skip an important concept, or fail to explain it sufficiently, you can always step in. The multiplayer classroom takes more planning in what we call the preproduction stage. But once the game is released (when students are playing it), all of that work pays off in classes that are more fun for you, as well as the students, without sacrificing the quality of the learning experience.

CONDUCT

One section found in all of the syllabi that I have not touched on yet is conduct. As a professional writer, I am very cognizant of the power of the pen, or the spoken word, over the sword. In our increasingly uncivil society, one of the first beachheads of the war on civility is the classroom. Students from all walks of life enter with their own perceptions of appropriate behavior and discourse nurtured by their homes and peers.

Multiplayer games from *World of Warcraft* to the multiplayer mode of first-person shooters allow audible chat. Players speak to one another through microphones and headphones either facilitated by external software, or within the game itself. This serves two purposes. The first: Orders to fellow players on a team can be delivered much faster, a necessity in boss raids and when battling other teams of human players. The second was introduced on the previous level: trash talking.

Have a listen to trash talking and l33t speak, and you might think gamers would seem to be a peer group at odds with civil conduct in the classroom. Yet guild cultures are built from the top down. The leadership of a guild has the power to regulate the boundaries of discourse, and they do. Many of the largest guilds in MMOs have in their memberships gamers drawn from the widest possible spectrum of political, social, racial, cultural, and geographical groups.

The best leaders acknowledge that what may be proper language for American teenage boys may not be appropriate for senior citizens from Japan. So they lay down rules for both behavior and discourse. Players *want* rules, and the rules must be clear and concise.

An article in *Time* magazine prompted by the end of Hosni Mubarak's 30-year reign in Egypt, "What Was Mubarak Thinking? Inside the Mind of a Dictator," highlights the work of biological anthropologist Chris Boehm at the University of Southern California: "[Boehm] studies the human revolutionary impulse and has been struck in particular by how it plays to a unique tension in the psychology of our species. On the one hand, humans are extremely hierarchical primates, readily picking leaders and assenting to their authority for the larger good of the community. On the other hand, our hunter-gatherer ancestors were a very egalitarian bunch, doing best when the group operated collectively, with dominance asserted only subtly."

Good guilds survive and prosper because it is human nature to seek out leaders, but members want to feel that their voices are heard. Bad guilds fail when their leaders become totalitarian. Because guilds are made up of members who, whatever their backgrounds, seek a common success and style of play, they routinely allow themselves to be led. And they self-police. This style of play is right at home in the multiplayer classroom.

One final thought: Guild leaders have the power to discipline and even remove members. Schools have the same power. But everyone uses these measures as a last resort. To gamers, self-policing and a willingness to follow the rules are second nature.

One of the features of the multiplayer classroom is that the students engage in collaborative, as well as competitive, activities. Students are not focused entirely on their individual grades. They are given opportunities to help their guild mates and other students in the class. Working together on the final projects is an obvious example, and it has been a part of classrooms long before any of them became multiplayer. We will see a couple more examples in a minute when we get to the multiplayer version of "Multiplayer Game Design."

THE 2010 SYLLABUS

It is time we had a look at the Spring 2010 syllabus of "Multiplayer Game Design," as shown in Figure 5.2.

The syllabus for the second multiplayer classroom is very similar to the first. The main difference was the shift from all video games to multiplayer games, specifically persistent worlds. This class did not focus on the multiplayer versions of solo-player games.

The XP leveling was the same with the same faults we discussed on Level 3. The methods of crafting and selling game ideas, forming guilds, and so on, were the same. And students would again be responsible for quests, presenting reading material in class.

Topics for crafted papers were made more suitable for the focus of the new class. Students reported on an MMO article, analyzed an MMO-based research topic, and crafted a longer analysis of an MMO of their choice. This could be one they were already playing, or one they started soon after beginning the class.

The first major change—to the five reading quizzes, or "random mobs"—was another chance for players to help their guild mates, but this was an ad hoc choice I made after the semester had started. We will have a look at it on the next level.

Solo camping remained the same on the first iteration of the syllabus, but unfortunately (or fortunately, depending upon your point of view), our main text, Richard Bartle's *Designing Virtual Worlds*, and my own *Character Development and Storytelling for Games*, were much better edited than *Understanding Video Games*.

Camping

Camping means remaining in a single geographical location to repeatedly farm a mob each time one spawns.

Indiana University, Bloomington
Department of Telecommunications

T366: Multiplayer Game Design

Section 13353
Spring 2010
MW 11:15-12:30pm
Room 226 RTV Building

Instructor: Lee Sheldon
Office: Room 311 RTV Building
Phone: 855-6840
Office Hours: MW 10:00-11:00am
Email: clsheldo@indiana.edu

Prerequisites: Permission of Instructor

Description
Focus is on massively-multiplayer online games and virtual worlds. Students will be introduced to the design elements and production requirements necessary to create and maintain online games. We will study various existing worlds from major commercial worlds like *World of Warcraft* to free web-based games.

Format
This class is designed as a multiplayer game.

Class time will be divided between fighting monsters (Quizzes, Exams etc.), completing quests (Presentations of Games, Research etc.) and crafting (Personal Game Premises, Game Analysis Papers, Video Game Concept Document etc.).

At the beginning of the semester everyone in the class will choose and name their avatars. The first task is to craft the premise of a multiplayer game you would like to design. Guilds to craft these games will be chosen, balanced as closely as possible by l33t skillz and interests. Guilds will choose their names. There will be six guilds of six-seven members each depending upon final class size.

Grading Procedure
You will begin on the first day of class as a Level One avatar. Level Twelve is the highest level you can achieve:

Level	XP*	Letter Grade
Level Twelve	1860	A
Level Eleven	1800	A-
Level Ten	1740	B+
Level Nine	1660	B
Level Eight	1600	B-
Level Seven	1540	C+
Level Six	1460	C

Level Five	1400	C-
Level Four	1340	D+
Level Three	1260	D
Level Two	1200	D-
Level One	0	F

*Your level will be determined by experience points (XP) on a 2000 XP scale. You gain XP by defeating mobs, completing quests and crafting.

- Solo: Craft your own game proposal. (Written, 50 pts.)
- Solo: Present your game proposal to the class. (25 pts.)
- Solo: Sell your game proposal to the class. (**Extra credit**. 25 pts.)
- Raid: Guild reading presentation (75 pts. each person, 1 of these per guild)

- Pick-Up Group: 2-Player reading presentation (150 pts. each person, cannot team with fellow guild member) **OR**
- Solo: 1-Player reading presentation (150 pts. but easier than above)

- Solo: Craft 3 page report on MMO article (Written, 75 pts.)
- Solo: Craft 3 page analysis of MMO-based research topic (Written, 100 pts.)
- Solo: Craft 5 page analysis on MMO of your choice (Written, 125 pts.)
- Solo: Defeat Five Random Mobs (5 written reading quizzes, 250 pts. total, 1 **extra credit** question per quiz)
- Solo: Defeat Level Boss (Midterm Exam, 400 pts.)
- Guild: Paper Prototype Presentation (50 pts. each)
- Guild: Craft Final Project: Video Game Concept (Written, 400 pts.)
- Solo: Class attendance (300 skill pts. total, 10 to start. 290 additional pts. at 10 pts. per day of attendance)
- **Extra credit** for early completion of final proposal (10 pts./Monday; 5 pts./Tuesday; see calendar)
- Solo Camping: Text editing (**Extra credit**. 1 pt. per mistake. 50 pt. cap per player. First come first served. Each mob only spawns once.)
- Group: Peer Review Secret Ballot (**Extra credit**. 0-100 possible XP as follows:)
    1. Guild Leader 100 pts.
    2. Raid Leader 75 pts.
    3. Solid Guild Crafter 50 pts.
    4. Needs Rez 25 pts.
    5. Leroy Jenkins 0 pts.

Grading is rigorous. Spelling, grammar and punctuation must be proofed. Points will be deducted otherwise.

Attendance and Conduct

You are expected to attend every class. Assignments are due at the *beginning* of every class. Late assignments will subtract from the grade for that assignment, one half letter grade for each day the assignment is late.

Plagiarism, submitting assignments written by others, and other forms of academic misconduct are governed by university policy. In a word: DON'T.

Classroom conduct: Participate with civility and an abiding appreciation for the power of words. Respect others, even those who hold opposing views.

Required Text

Designing Virtual Worlds. Richard Bartle.
Character Development and Storytelling for Games. Lee Sheldon.

Suggested Reading

Developing Online Games. Mulligan and Petrovsky.
Massively Multiplayer Game Development. Thor Alexander et al.
Synthetic Worlds. Edward Castronova.
Community Building on the Web. Amy Jo Kim
My Tiny Life: Crime and Passion in a Virtual World. Julian Dibbell
A Theory of Fun. Raph Koster
Flow: The Psychology of Optimal Experience. Mihaly Csikszentmihalyi.

Figure 5.2
Spring 2010 syllabus.

Instead, players helped build a glossary of MMO terms. The first player to suggest a term and definition received one point of XP.

The other change was replacing François' "Waste of Rations" with "Leroy Jenkins" when describing a guild member who contributed nothing to the final concept document. Leroy Jenkins was by far a more appropriate choice for MMOs, even though I apparently misspelled his first name. It is supposed to be "Leeroy."

Leeroy Jenkins

Leeroy Jenkins was an avatar created by *World of Warcraft* player Ben Schulz. Leeroy, absent from his computer while the complex strategy at the beginning of a major boss raid was discussed, returns and impatiently charges on his own, resulting in a wipe of the entire raid. Videos of the raid can be found on YouTube. There has been some discussion as to whether or not the video was staged.

Leeroy's name, misspelled or not, has entered the realm of legend on the Internet—beyond even MMO players or other video gamers (see Table 5.1). Clearly, whether the record of his deed was staged or not, his name deserves to honor those who fail to contribute positively to their guild's efforts.

How did the actual class differ from the syllabus? More than I expected. How did this second iteration of the multiplayer classroom work? Much better than I could have dreamed.

Here are the real-world terms in this chapter that map directly to game terms. You will notice that there are fewer, and we'll do away with tables now that we have most of the necessary terminology mapped.

Table 5.1 Terminology Map

Building a Glossary	Camping
Non-Contributing Team Member	Leeroy Jenkins

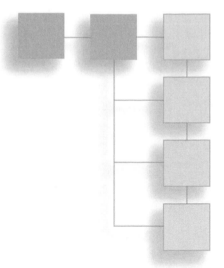

LEVEL 6

MULTIPLAYER GAME DESIGN CLASS

"Multiplayer Game Design" was taught in the Radio/TV Center on the Indiana University, Bloomington campus. The Department of Telecommunications, where I was an assistant professor, is housed there, as are WTIU, the PBS television station, and WFIU, its sister radio station. They serve over 20 counties in western and south-central Indiana. Completed in 1963, the building has been upgraded several times over the years and now features broadband, remote conferencing facilities, sound stages, and HD video equipment. Projects I contemplated, but never had time to explore in this media candy store, included dramatic TV and radio shows that would have returned me to my first career: writing and producing television.

Unfortunately, there was one drawback with the upgraded facilities. The furniture in Room 226, where I taught a number of classes, was not nearly as flexible as the older-style classroom in Ballantine (see Figure 6.1). Gone were the chair desks, replaced by melamine tables not really conducive to lugging around—a fact I learned early on when I assisted in turning the room from a classroom into a square of tables for faculty meetings.

When word got out about the first multiplayer classroom, we had students asking to sit in at least for a class or two. When students heard another multiplayer class would be offered in the spring, we had to turn people away. As it was, Room 226 also was not built to handle the 40 students we managed to cram in. Every chair in Figure 6.1 was filled.

Figure 6.1
RTV Room 226.

With students locked into rows, the zones could not be as elegantly separated as in the Ballantine classroom where guilds could maneuver chairs to speak to one another, or where opposing guilds could face off in intellectual PvP battles. Instead, members of the six guilds—four with seven members, two with six— would each be clustered together in a couple of rows that were designated as zones.

ZONES

These zones were named after prominent designers of virtual worlds.

- **Dungeon of Bartle.** Named for Richard Bartle. In addition to writing our primary text, Bartle was co-designer with Roy Trubshaw of MUD, the first virtual world in 1979.

- **Garriott Gardens.** Named after Richard Garriott, designer of the Ultima series of role-playing games. *Ultima 4* was notable as one of the first solo games to feature moral choices, which affected the development of the player's avatar. *Ultima Online*, released in 1997, was the first MMO to truly earn the title "massive" with over 100,000 players at its peak.

- **Caverns of Koster.** Raph Koster, one of the creators of the text MUD, *Legend MUD*, became lead designer on *Ultima Online* and then creative director on *Star Wars: Galaxies*, released in 2003.

- **Sellers' Cellars.** Mike Sellers was one of the founders of Archetype Interactive, developers of the first 3D MMO, *Meridian 59*, released by 3DO in 1996.

- **Wright City.** Will Wright is best known for the Sims franchise of stand-alone games. He is one of the most visionary game designers working today. His contribution to virtual worlds was *Sims Online*, released in 2002.

- **Pardo's Peak.** Rob Pardo, currently vice president of game design at Blizzard Entertainment, was the lead designer of *World of Warcraft*, released in 2004, the most successful MMO to date.

Mud

Mud was originally an acronym for *multi-user dungeon,* later also used for *multi-user dimension* and *multi-user domain.* Muds are text-based virtual worlds, the precursors of MMOs, and they can still be found on the Internet today.

Again I moved guilds from zone to zone throughout the semester. Not only did it mean one group could not sit at the back of the room to text and avoid discussion all semester long, but it also figured more prominently in the gameplay. Now they were required to answer questions concerning each of the people the zones were named after for extra credit.

ROLES

After everyone chose avatar names and pitched their game ideas to the class, they voted to determine the top six they would be crafting concept documents for. I again asked for them to give me a list of what roles they each wanted to play. I still drew the names of the roles from regular game development. Because the class was larger than the previous one, I added one position for all guilds, and a second for the larger guilds. Four guilds were made up of seven members. Two contained six.

I then spent several hours sifting through their choices of games they wanted to work on and the roles they wanted to play. As before, I started with Designer,

Producer, Writer, Art Lead, and Tech Lead. I added Customer Service to all since MMOs are much more of an ongoing service than stand-alone video games. I left the seventh position up to the discretion of the four larger guilds. They chose Audio Lead.

This process of balancing the guilds is one of the most difficult tasks I faced, although I'd had the same challenge in the iterations of the classes before they became multiplayer. Whether you ask them to list three or seven games or roles, the key is to try and give everyone either his or her top first or second choice. Only a couple of students ended up with a lower choice in one category. I made certain that they received their number one choice in the other. So, if I had to give them their last choice of game, I saw to it that they had their first choice of role. A few also received second choices in both. After some initial shrugs and scowls, this system was accepted, and no complaints were heard or excuses made later about what they were assigned. Table 6.1 lists the guild names they chose and the titles of the MMOs they would design.

I confess I cannot find a list of avatar names for this class in my files. If any students from the class read this book, please publish your avatar names in the forums attached to the "Gaming the Classroom" blog at *http://gamingtheclass-room.wordpress.com/*. If there's a new printing of this book, I'll include them!

Table 6.1 Guilds and Virtual Worlds

Guild	Virtual World
Kings of Cosmos	*Cosmos*
The Posse	*Crime World*
Stomping Puppies	*Infestation*
Guild-a-Bear	*Musique*
Beast Knees	*Reign of Beast*
WTF	*Triad*

MMOs and Community

Several interesting ideas for MMOs emerged in this class. *Musique* was a hybrid of a rhythm-based music game like *Rock Band* and *Guitar Hero* and a story-driven, massively multiplayer role-playing game. *Cosmos* was a Facebook game that offered players the chance to not only explore the universe, but also to create new worlds. It impressed the industry guests I brought in as boss mobs enough that they were interested in actually making the game.

Quests in the class were again presentations: solo, pick-up groups from different guilds, and guild presentations. The pick-up groups were important. Because they were undertaken only by players in different guilds, they were an opportunity for players to work with other players they were not used to. This helped foster a sense of community in the class as a whole. Community is a very important word in MMO design.

Also, guild quests did not require all guild members to participate. One member could have presented, and all guild members would have shared in the XP. No guild has ever chosen to do any variation of this in any of the multiplayer classes. All guilds chose to evenly divide up the labors. Whether this was due to the attitude, "If I have to do this, we all will." Or if was from a sense of fairness or solidarity, I don't know.

In MMOs, players will discover a new technique to defeat a difficult mob, the most lucrative items to craft and sell, the location of NPCs necessary to complete a quest, and so on. They will then share this information either within the game or on Internet forums dedicated to the game. In the "Theory and Practice of Game Design" class, I planned to hide some quiz answers, taped to the bottom of chairs in each zone. Students would still have had to match the answers to the questions, but they would have been encouraged to trade the information with one another. I felt this would foster classroom discussion and interaction, even from those who would not easily take part. Plus, it would aid in general community building.

Some torn ligaments prevented me from getting across campus from my screenwriting class to "Theory and Practice of Game Design" fast enough to beat the students to the room. If anybody saw me planting clues, the game would have been up, so I tabled the idea. I have yet to try this again, but I think it would reward the effort required.

QUIZZES AND INNOVATIVE PRESENTATIONS

I allowed the class to vote on the type of random mob reading quizzes they wanted. PvP, with the guilds taking turns answering questions selected by a die roll, was preferred by the class to the usual solo written quiz, with only one exception. This student was in both of the first two multiplayer classrooms. She pointed out that once her guild discovered she read and studied diligently, they could all relax. Still, other guild members occasionally were able to come to her aid.

How did the switch from farming typos and mistakes in the "Theory and Practice of Game Design" class to glossary building in "Multiplayer Game Design" work out? Not so well. Players were pleased to prove their knowledge was greater than the textbook's. And the exercise of finding the mistakes forced them to read carefully and learn some spelling and grammar along the way. The glossary proved to be little more than tapping into their firsthand knowledge or collecting data from the Internet. Unfortunately, books with so many errors are hard to come by! I used glossary building only one more time.

As before, the reading presentation quests were delivered to the class by their fellow students, with questions and comments from me. Again, these players relied on PowerPoint for the most part. I was determined not to repeat the last class, which often read their bulleted lists aloud. So I coached them on how to deliver PowerPoint talks and to find new and innovative approaches. Most students began supplementing their talks with illustrations drawn on the whiteboard and YouTube videos, as a few had before.

Then a breakthrough: One guild, Guild-a-Bear, built their presentation as a game! They started with a sophisticated PowerPoint template found on the Jefferson County Schools in Dandridge, Tennessee website, credited to Mark E. Damon. They would present two or three slides and then seamlessly switch to a version of *So You Want to Be a Millionaire?*—where players would race to answer multiple-choice questions based on the small slice of material they had just covered. Winners got candy. They had the full attention of their classmates for an hour. It was awesome! Another guild, The Posse, wrote a script for part of the presentation and acted it out. Beautiful!

It's important to note that in both cases, the material covered was clearly presented. Because of the uniqueness of the presentations, retention seemed to be improved as well. On the midterm, the material covered by *So You Want to Be a Millionaire?* was nailed by almost everyone who had been present on the day of the game.

But what about that candy? That's clearly an extrinsic reward. What does that mean exactly? I like the clarity of this explanation from the *ChangingMinds.org* website.

Extrinsic Motivation

"Extrinsic motivation is when I am motivated by external factors, as opposed to the internal drivers of intrinsic motivation. Extrinsic motivation drives me to do things for tangible rewards or pressures, rather than for the fun of it.

When I do something, I have to explain why I do it. If I am being rewarded extrinsically for doing it, then I can explain to myself that I am doing it for the reward. In this way, rewards can decrease internal motivation as people work to gain the reward rather than because they like doing the work or believe it is a good thing to do.

In effect, extrinsic motivations can change a pleasurable into work."

The year 2010 has seen the widespread adoption of the new concept I alluded to on Level 1: gamification. As I mentioned then, quite by accident I discovered that I was apparently doing it.

Gamification

Simply put, gamification is the application of game mechanics to non-game activities. Its underlying idea is to increase engagement. It is invading all types of marketing. The first Gamification Summit was held in January 2011. It can, and probably should to be successful, include both extrinsic and intrinsic motivation.

As Jesse Schell points out in his talk, we are being bombarded by extrinsic rewards to modify our behavior from choosing a certain product to making healthier decisions (see Figure 6.2). Yet, critics rightfully point out that extrinsic rewards are not always the best form of motivation. By focusing attention on the reward instead of the action that triggers it, motivation is removed when the reward is removed. That may be fine for the duration of the *So You Want to Be a Millionaire?* game the students played in class. It may not be so fine for the long term.

MIDTERM EXAM

One of the major successes of this version of the MC was the preparation for our first boss raid (midterm exam). I came up with 60 questions (40 would be used on the exam), and we had a guild vs. guild PvP session.

Figure 6.2
Extrinsic motivation anyone?

Here are the *only* rules I gave them:

1. Each guild could only use a single copy of each of the classes' two textbooks.

2. They were allowed to look up answers in the books, *but they were required to close books* before answering.

3. Guilds won the privilege of answering by shouting out their zone name ("hitting the buzzer") to answer a question.

4. The questions on the midterm would be in the order they were covered in class. For this prep, I jumped around through the 60 questions.

At first, the person holding the book containing the answer would immediately memorize the answer, slam the book closed, and shout out their guild name. This worked fine for the first few questions, deliberately chosen for their simplicity. Most only required a word or two to answer. The students who had done the most reading were fastest at finding answers. In this way, the exercise was designed like leveling in an MMO. The questions got harder as we progressed. And one person attempting to memorize became problematic when faced with answers requiring multiple elements.

The player with the book would begin confidently, start to stumble, and end up looking sheepish when trying to instantly memorize a list of up to eight items, each composed of a sentence or two. (I did reduce the elements required in an answer to two or three on the actual exam. I believe I've already stated I'm not quite that sadistic.)

How did the guilds cope? One guild divided up the elements among their guild mates. So the one with the book would find it, show it quickly to each member in turn, and they would shout out their zone name. Then each member, in turn, would answer with the one item she or he had memorized.

So pretty soon all of the guilds were dividing up the elements, one person taking only one. A couple of the guilds were better at this than the others. So the guilds that weren't winning were forced to find a new tactic.

Finally, one guild realized that writing down the answers, or at least enough to aid memory, was faster than swinging the book around, showing members the answer in the book, making sure they had it, and then moving to the next. That guild dominated only a couple of times before the others caught on and duplicated their technique.

Three or four of the guilds were now neck-and-neck. It would take yet another inspiration from one to finally triumph.

At last, a member of the winning guild took out a cell phone and photographed the page found by the member who had done the most reading. The other guilds called foul! That was cheating! But I pointed out that the rules said nothing about using cell phones. So, for the last few questions all guilds were using cell phones to simply photograph the needed page and then read from the photos.

I then pointed out to them that changing their strategies and tactics was exactly how guilds learn to defeat mobs in their boss raids, learning from their wipes, modifying their approach, until at last they bring down the beast.

This was the best class that semester. They had a great time competing and trash talking. I had a great time watching the essential core of the multiplayer classroom blossom, seeing them learn the way they learned in games, by failure, and then getting up, brushing themselves off, and trying again.

The winners received no XP. There was no extrinsic reward. There was, however, a very important intrinsic reward. Here again is a great explanation from *ChangingMinds.org*.

Intrinsic Motivation

"Intrinsic motivation is when I am motivated by internal factors, as opposed to the external drivers of extrinsic motivation. Intrinsic motivation drives me to do things just for the fun of it, or because I believe it is a good or right thing to do."

What was the intrinsic reward for the PvP midterm prep (see Figure 6.3)? They had a great time learning. They had fun playing together. And the lasting extrinsic reward? The vast majority of the class did extremely well on the midterm, far better than *any* major exam I had given up until then, including in the first multiplayer classroom. All except three students earned a huge chunk of XP.

Figure 6.3
Intrinsic motivation comes from within!

The debate between extrinsic and intrinsic rewards will continue. Clouding the issue is the fact that extrinsic rewards can have positive effects. As

ChangingMinds.org points out, "When you want them to stop doing something: first give them extrinsic rewards for doing the unwanted behavior, then remove the reward." And intrinsic rewards can have negative effects such as the "Over-justification Effect." *ChangingMinds.org* one last time.

Over-Justification Effect

"This occurs where I attribute my behavior more to a conspicuous extrinsic motivator than to intrinsic reasons."

What should be clear is that the multiplayer classroom comes with both extrinsic and intrinsic rewards, just as MMOs do. And it can be just as compelling.

Again, since each guild member received the same grade for the concept document, I added a secret ballot peer review, so that anyone not contributing would receive a weighted grade. And again, I was concerned that they would simply give each other equally high marks or that personal animosity might factor in. Yet, again, I saw no evidence of either in their rankings. The assessments they made coincided with my own observations.

"Multiplayer Game Design" was the last class I taught at Indiana University. The preceding winter I had been approached by two schools seeking to expand their video game programs. This came at a time when I was increasingly frustrated by the lack of growth in the program at IU. In the end, the chance to help build an already top-ranked program took me to Rensselaer Polytechnic Institute in Troy, New York. I took the multiplayer classroom with me.

STUDENT EVALUATION QUOTES

Here is a balanced sample of official quotes from students:

"The learning environment was outstanding."

"It was fairly structured. I liked how we were able to teach each other."

"I loved the environment because we learned by playing games and having hands-on material."

"Class is full of like-minded people that enjoy video games as much as I do, so I would say the environment was great."

"The learning environment is fun and interactive."

"Horrible. He didn't teach us anything. All the lectures were done by other students. Also, his descriptions of assignments resembled: "Write a three-page paper about games.""

"Erratic but enjoyable."

"I liked how the class was set up like a game. Made it more interesting."

"Lee, you're the expert, we want to hear you lecture, not the class!"

"Heavily applicable to the real world/actual small team development groups."

"The learning environment is great. It's a new class design that worked out, and not everyone wants to teach how this class was taught."

"The learning environment was great, low-key, and welcoming."

"Fun, easy-going, and critical."

"It is very much a self-taught class. We would do presentations over [course material], which is kind of a good idea. By reading and having to explain it to your peers, you understand and retain the information better. That being said... I would have loved to hear Lee talk. He has vast amounts of wisdom concerning this subject, and he is also not boring to listen to. But I am, and so are most of my peers. I didn't want for them to teach me."

"Lee-tastic."

Case History 2

University of Arizona South: Teaching with Technology

Wayne Brent, PhD

Senior Consultant at the Office of Instruction and Assessment

University of Arizona

Tucson, Arizona

Max Lieberman

Student in Educational Technology M.S. program

University of Arizona South

Tucson, Arizona

Connie Hackathorn

Student in Educational Technology M.S. program

University of Arizona South

Tucson, Arizona

Figure CH2.1
Connie Hackathorn, Max Lieberman, and Wayne Brent.

Case History 2 involves a team experience from Wayne Brent, Max Lieberman, and Connie Hackathorn that is still developing (see Figure CH2.1). Following you'll see the second version of the case history that they submitted. So far, they have been successful enough to name their method: "Game Attributes and Mechanics in Education," or GAME. Never discount the advantage of a good acronym!

Students Max Lieberman and Connie Hackathorn were given the assignment of adapting an existing course into a game. They approached this challenge with formal game design methodology, and not surprisingly, introduced technology into the design with great success.

They pared down an initially complex design so that the game would not overwhelm the learning, retaining achievements and skill points as core mechanics. Here is the current state of the GAME.

THE SETUP

In the summer of 2010, we were two then-graduate students at the University of Arizona. We were offered a unique opportunity: Help Wayne, Brent, a faculty member, adapt his existing graduate course on "Teaching with Technology" into a game. At our disposal, we had our knowledge, enthusiastic support from

Dr. Brent, and assistance from his department, including limited access to a talented programmer. Despite a short timeframe—the course needed to be ready for the following semester—we leapt at this chance. The game-based course design that resulted is now in its second semester of use, and our team continues to iterate on our technology and methodology. We call this design "Game Attributes and Mechanics in Education," or GAME. We are currently making plans to support instructors in other fields who want to adopt the GAME model at the University of Arizona and beyond.

The Team

Wayne Brent, Ph.D., Senior Consultant at the Office of Instruction and Assessment, University of Arizona

Wayne is the instructor of record for the Graduate College course, "Teaching with Technology." His broad background in applied educational theory, assessment, and emerging technologies—and his willingness to implement a promising but experimental design—made our project possible. The Office of Instruction and Assessment was an ideal home for this project, and it provided us with access to resources that proved critical to implement our ambitious design.

Max Lieberman, student in Educational Technology M.S. program, University of Arizona

Connie Hackathorn, student in Educational Technology M.S. program, University of Arizona

As final-semester M.S. students in a program with a strong focus on both pedagogy and technology, we (Max and Connie) took an active role in course design and construction, participated in weekly class sessions, and interacted with students online. Max focused primarily on game design and LMS integration, while Connie addressed learner-centered teaching and rubric development. Both have remained involved with GAME since their graduation.

The Course (Before)

Dr. Brent had taught "Teaching with Technology" for several years in a blended classroom/online learning environment. The course was supplemented by a

Learning Management System (LMS), as well as by many of the emerging technologies that are covered within the class.

"Teaching with Technology" was designed to encourage "mastery learning," meaning that students would acquire skills and content expertise and an ability to reflect metacognitively on what was being learned. The course was perhaps unusual in the sheer breadth of content that it endeavored to cover. The most recent non-game–based version of the course featured more than 30 modules of content in areas including applied learning and teaching theory, classroom management, educational technology, assessment and evaluation, and techniques for collaboration.

WHY A GAME?

Our reasons for turning "Teaching with Technology" into a game were grounded in earlier theoretical and practical academic work on video games in education. Well-designed games provide integrated assessment and contextual feedback; they are good at keeping players motivated and in flow; they incorporate established pedagogical techniques including scaffolded instruction, variable ratio reinforcement, and social learning. Searching for connections between game mechanics and learning theory, we looked to authors including James Paul Gee, David Shaffer, Kurt Squire, and Marc Prensky. Lee Sheldon and Dr. Janna Jackson provided models for bringing game mechanics into the very structure of the course.

We hoped to move beyond the previously published research by integrating LMS functionality into our course. With an LMS, we could partly automate grading, track various data on student behavior, and export this information in a standardized format. This would allow us to visualize student progress in game-like ways. Although it took some time to arrive at the initial working version of our course "dashboard," we knew from the start that we wanted to provide students with a digital "character sheet."

Our goals included improving student engagement in the course, providing students with new tools to improve the reflection process, offering more frequent and contextual feedback, and giving students more freedom to forge their own path through the material.

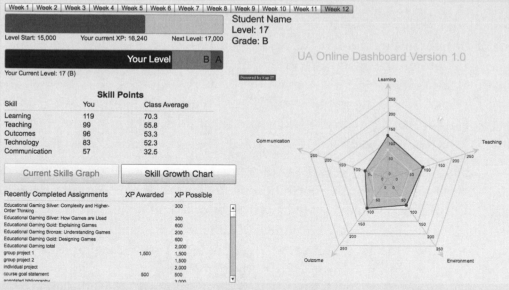

Figure CH2.2
Version 1 of the GAME dashboard, featuring grade, assignment completion, and skill point information, created by programmer Gary Carstensen for the University of Arizona team. Future revisions will bring more LMS functions into the dashboard interface.

GAME Design

As a team, we had a great deal of experience with teaching and technology, but only one member had any background in game design. We proceeded slowly and deliberately, talking about the implications of each decision and referring to examples from previous research and from commercial games. The initial workflow, over the summer of 2010, went something like this:

- Take notes on similar projects and on game mechanics that could fit into the format of a graduate-level course.

- Choose two or three mechanics and develop them into something that might work for us.

- Realize that this was madness and would not work for a previously unconsidered reason.

- Wash, rinse, repeat.

Game design is never easy. It gets even harder when you consider the effect of each choice not just on the game as a game—*Is this more or less fun? More or less balanced?*—but on the experience of students and an instructor, for whom what is learned, and how well, must remain the primary measures of success. At the same time, we wanted to avoid what Richard Van Eck identified as the main pitfall of many games created by educators: that "neither the learning nor the game is effective or engaging."

We wanted to find ways to exploit the extrinsic motivational power of games without limiting the intrinsic motivation of students to learn. We considered it critical to focus on mechanics, which were not only compatible with a learner-centered instructional model, but inherently aligned with one. There needed to be no question of the game somehow "overshadowing" the learning; to as great an extent as possible, they needed to be the same thing.

Previous course-as-game models adopted the framework of a traditional role-playing game (RPG), and after some deliberation we realized that an RPG was a wise choice. RPGs feature complex numeric metaphors for character progression, which could be adapted to serve as both a grading system and a tool for student reflection. The genre is also fairly flexible, which allowed us to incorporate mechanics adapted from elsewhere.

GAME is a design-based research project, which means that we expect our technology and pedagogy to continually evolve based on our experiences and observations. Our current design for GAME (now in its second semester) features some elements taken from other game-based courses. We use a system similar to Lee Sheldon's for grading, in which experience points and levels correspond to letter grades. Janna Jackson's policy of allowing students to retry assignments for a higher score was also adopted. We have also incorporated several additional game-like systems:

- **Multiple assignments within each content area, each mapped to Bloom's Taxonomy.** Students must complete lower-level assignments within a module in order to progress to more challenging and valuable assignments. These assignments are designated as "Bronze (identify, remember, understand, apply)," "Silver (analyze, evaluate, critique, summarize)," or "Gold (compose, create, design, plan, invent)" and are partly inspired by both difficulty levels and linear progression in video games.

- **A course planning tool that offers students a tremendous amount of student choice about what to study and how to study it.** This tool enables students to select from hundreds of available assignments in dozens of content areas, using an intuitive drag-and-drop interface. Potential XP and skill point totals are automatically calculated so that students can see what they can expect to achieve in the areas of grading, knowledge, and skills by the end of the course. This tool also allows us to review students' plans of study and provide feedback and guidance before they are finalized. Together with our assignment level system, the planning tool provides students with a guided experience through the sandbox structure of "Teaching with Technology."

- **"Achievements" recognizing accomplishments such as exceptional performance on a specific assignment, aggregate skill point totals, and so on.** Similar systems exist in many games and game platforms, most notably on Xbox Live. Our achievements are awarded based on data collected automatically by the LMS. Students are notified that they have earned an achievement by email.

- **Skill points, which are awarded in five categories corresponding to key course themes and skills.** Students' individual skill point distributions reflect what they choose to study within the course competencies, and serve as a resource as students reflect metacognitively on the learning process. We devised several secret achievements to recognize particular patterns of skill point distributions, such as "Jack of All Trades" and "One-Track Mind."

One of the main strengths of this design is that it incorporates many of the benefits of game-based learning without sacrificing either flexibility (the framework is viable for many subjects and student populations) or applicability in a traditional educational context (real schools can do this with real educators). By organizing content into modules, we are able to gate progress, so that students cannot move beyond their level of expertise—as in a video game, assessment is built into the activity. At the same time, the thematic connections between modules help students to generalize knowledge beyond situated meanings and ensure that learners are supported along the path to mastery, even if the goal at the end of that path changes during the semester.

PRACTICAL CHALLENGES AND SOLUTIONS

Our enrollment for the initial GAME-based semester of "Teaching with Technology" was small, numbering only six students. This allowed us to spend time evaluating the reaction of individual students to the course format. Ours was a diverse group: students from the humanities and the hard sciences; from the United States and China; students who had gone right from college to graduate school; and others who were on their second and third careers. Some students were taking the class as credit toward a UA Certificate in College Teaching.

There was no guarantee that our students would have prior experience with video games or RPGs, or even a liking for games in general. To make things even more interesting, we did not publicize the course format until the first day of class. In general, students were receptive and even eager to engage with this new challenge. While they lacked experience with games, many of our students were actively interested in learning and teaching theories and could understand the rationale for the course design in those terms.

The LMS provided our first major challenge. Designed to present content sequentially, it was ill-suited to a course structure in which modules and assignments were listed hierarchically in four subject areas. Students had trouble finding the modules and assignments they were interested in. We were able to address this issue by providing an alternate content overview, in the form of a visual course map, as shown in Figure CH2.3 This course map has since been improved to let students access assignments directly, allowing them to circumvent the traditional LMS view if they want.

Other issues were more fundamental to the design of the course. Two weeks into the first semester with GAME, one student asked how the ability to choose from so many assignments might affect class discussions. ("How will we have anything in common to talk about?") This proved not to be a problem for our course, both because strong thematic connections existed between the superficially disparate content modules, and frankly, because Dr. Brent is adept at directing classroom discussions. However, it is a valid concern for other implementations of a similarly open course design. Our current GAME implementation specifies weekly topics for class discussion, while allowing enough flexibility to address issues related to specific assignments as they arise.

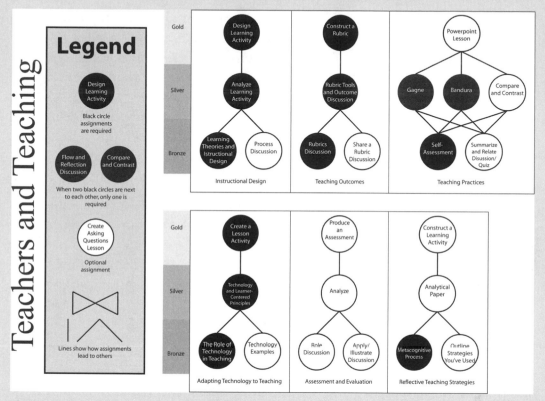

Figure CH2.3
A portion of the revised "Teaching with Technology" course map dealing with "teachers and teaching," featuring an overview of the assignments contained within six of the 30+ content modules.

At the same time that there was concern that our course might be too open, we discovered that aspects of it were more closed than we had anticipated in that first semester. Required assignments ended up consuming more time than expected, offering students too little freedom to chart their own path through the content. Our second semester course features far fewer required assignments, as well as rebalanced XP and skill point valuations for each assignment. The course planning tool was also integrated into the dashboard between semesters. The result has been a more appropriate workload for students and more opportunity for students to motivate themselves by pursuing intrinsic interests.

FUTURE PLANS

Our first implementation of GAME was a success. Students readily took to the online dashboard, which allowed them to see at a glance how close they were to the grade they wanted, and what assignments were still available to help them get there. Procrastinators could see that their skill point totals were lagging behind their classmates', and overachievers knew when they were far enough ahead of the game to take a breather. In an exciting example of emergent gameplay, one student earned enough experience points to skip the final project entirely. We also observed a great deal of metacognitive reflection. Students were thinking about what they were learning, and about how they were learning it.

One of the students who at first resisted our game-based design ended up excelling in the course, as did several who accepted the course design immediately. Very few students struggled, and although we have taken steps to prevent similar problems in the future, these struggles were mainly unrelated to GAME. The integration of tried-and-true game mechanics into our class didn't prove a panacea, but then we never expected it to. We have learned a tremendous amount from observing our ideas in practice.

As of this writing, we are in the middle of the second semester using GAME within "Teaching with Technology." We have already implemented many improvements to GAME, and we intend to continue iterating both in the short- and long-term. Specific plans include:

- Integrating more functions directly into the dashboard, which will improve instructor workflow as well as user experience.

- Experimenting with narrative elements to address the motivational component of "fantasy," as described by Thomas Malone.

- Creating meta-quests that encourage specific paths through course content using positive reinforcement (as an alternative to requiring specific assignments outright).

- Offering students new and different types of rewards, perhaps through an RPG-style skill tree.

- Building course management tools into an "educator view" within the dashboard.

We are confident that our positive results will be improved still further through continued iteration. Over time, we plan to expand the adoption of our game-based model to a wider group of teachers and a broader array of disciplines. Though no longer revolutionary, the idea of using games and game mechanics as serious educational tools is still new, and there is tremendous potential to conduct meaningful research on difficult questions. We are excited to be a part of this important field.

Those interested in following our efforts can do so at *http://gameua.wordpress. com*.

WORKS CITED

Jackson, Janna. "Game-Based Teaching: What Educators can Learn from Videogames." *Teaching Education* 20.3 (2009): 291–304.

Malone, Thomas. "What makes things fun to learn? Heuristics for designing instructional computer games." Proceedings of the 3rd ACM SIGSMALL symposium and the first SIGPC symposium on Small systems (1980) pp. 162–169.

Van Eck, Richard. "Digital Game-Based Learning: It's Not just the Digital Natives Who are Restless." *EDUCAUSE Review* 41.2 (2006): 20.

LEVEL 7

INTRODUCTION TO GAME DESIGN SYLLABUS

"Introduction to Game Design" was a first year, first semester course taught in the fall of 2010. Whereas my game design classes at Indiana University were predominantly upperclassmen and women, with a smattering of sophomores, almost the entire class at Rensselaer Polytechnic Institute were freshmen. There were other changes as well.

In the "Description of My Theory and Practice of Game Design" syllabus, I stated that the class was meant to cover both "game studies theory and video game design techniques," and we did. However, it was an uneasy mashup. The choice to combine the two was based on several factors.

I had been designing and writing video games for 15 years, yet I had never studied them formally. I learned first by playing them and then by making them. I was aware there was a growing body of research into many aspects of video games. In 2009, much of video game research had changed very little from previous decades, concentrating almost entirely on what are known as AAA titles.

AAA Game

While some people may like to suggest that AAA refers to games of high quality, in fact, it refers to video games produced by large teams with big budgets.

AAA games are played by the stereotypical hard-core gamer. AAA franchises that are so beloved by the hard-core are the following: *Halo, Grand Theft Auto, Madden NFL, Call of Duty, World of Warcraft, God of War, Gears of War*, and *Grapes of War*. Oh wait, that was *Grapes of Wrath*, and it was a book by John Steinbeck and a movie starring Henry Fonda. Sorry, I got carried away. If a gamer is someone who plays games, or even more narrowly, someone who plays video games, then what on earth is a hard-core gamer? Do they play naked? Well. . . yes, sometimes, but actually the term means something else.

Hard-Core Gamer

A hard-core gamer is someone playing games with complex rule sets and mechanics at the expense of most other essential activities such as work, relating to other humans, eating, sleeping, and so on.

Oh and yes, I confess that I am a borderline hard-core gamer, even if I have managed to wean myself from Red Bull, Fritos, and all-night boss raids. Well, I almost have. Yet, one thing should have been clear to researchers long before the Wii showed up in your granny's den. Games have never been solely for the stereotypical hard-core gamer.

We can trace the advent of casual video games back to 2006 when the Wii first captivated our grandparents; or 1997 when *Deer Hunter*, with its retro graphics and simplistic gameplay, charmed hunters out of their blinds; or 1990 when *Solitaire* was first included in Microsoft Windows; or even farther back into the dawn of all video games. *Pong* anyone?

And ever since the first casual game, we've had the stereotypical casual gamer.

Casual Gamer

A casual gamer is someone who doesn't mind the lower quality graphics, or the simplicity, or the fact that you can often finish a session of a casual game in a few minutes. In fact, casual gamers embrace all of these.

By 2009, we were well into what Jesper Juul documents and demystifies in his book, *A Casual Revolution*:

". . .a breathtaking moment in the history of video games. This is the moment in which the simplicity of early video games is being rediscovered, while new flexible designs are letting video games fit into the lives of players. Video games are being reinvented, and so is our image of those who play the games. This is the moment when we realize that everybody can be a video game player."

Casual games are not only simpler to play, but they are also far simpler and less expensive to produce. In the early days of computer games, the games came on floppy disks stuck in sandwich bags we called "baggies," actually a registered trademark of the Pactiv Corporation, but applied indiscriminately to all computer game packages. They were created by tiny teams of developers that ranged from a handful down to one.

Thanks to the iPhone and Facebook, games are again being built by teams as small as one. A graduate student of mine at Indiana University, Jenna Hoffstein, built an iPhone game, *Castaway Jelly*, with the GameSalad game builder from Gendai. She did everything, except the music.

THEORY AND DESIGN

So the first reason I taught both the theory and design was that I wanted to learn why the researchers were so focused on AAA titles meant for hard-core gamers. And I also wanted to bridge the gap between those of us who made the games and those who studied the end products of our labors. One question I still have not had adequately answered is this: Instead of theorizing about the developer's intent while designing a game, why not ask the developer?

I have never been asked why so many AAA game designs favor bullets over diplomacy. In spite of the elaborate theories about violent cultures and the bloodthirsty boys who have grown up to make bloodthirsty games, the answer is much simpler. Players of AAA titles demand instant feedback. Hit a button on the controller. The bullet immediately blasts the zombie's head to jelly. Instant feedback. Try to talk the terrorist out of killing civilians? Well, we still haven't figured that one out in the real world. All we know is there is no instant feedback.

Players of casual games, on the other hand, much to the surprise of many game designers, will docilely wait hours, even days, for the result of a key press. To grow a cantaloupe, you can't just shoot the ground.

Of course, game developers have all sorts of motives for why they *choose* to make yet another zombie game with exploding heads. I think it may be more productive to study the developers as much as our games. But, as I said, I have never been asked *any* questions about my morals, my parentage, or my motives.

Another reason why I combined the two is so I could bring myself up to speed on the field of game studies that has been growing so rapidly over the past two decades. I wanted to see through the eyes of those who studied games, rather than those who made them. So by committing to teaching game studies, I gave myself a pretty good reason to learn something about them.

A third reason was far more immediate and practical. Instructors qualified to teach anything about video games were thin on the ground at Indiana University. Apart from a few hardy pioneers, university-wide there was mild curiosity, but more overt skepticism about the need for video game classes. To many, they felt inconsequential, best left to trade schools, and not worthy of serious study. This was in large part due to the ideological struggle between professors who felt their mission was pure research, regardless of practical application, and those who thought teaching students the skills necessary to obtain jobs building things might be a valid pursuit as well. It is a tug-of-war playing out in universities all over the country.

Whatever the reason, we had far more students clamoring to learn about video games than we had instructors to teach them. It was necessary to take material that could be covered more reasonably in two courses and combine it into one.

At Rensselaer in "Introduction to Game Design," all I had to teach was one side of the coin. Practical knowledge about how to make video games would be enough.

THE 2010 FALL SYLLABUS

Here is the syllabus in Figure 7.1 to "Introduction to Game Design."

As you can see, the description reflects the narrower focus of the course: "game design and development."

Rensselaer Polytechnic Institute
Games and Simulation Arts and Sciences

67957: Introduction to Game Design

Section COGS-2520-03
Fall 2010
Days and Times TF 12-1:50pm
Room 2510 Sage Laboratory

Instructor: Lee Sheldon
Office: 4403 Sage Laboratory
Phone: 276-8264
Office Hours: TF 11-12
Email: sheldc2@rpi.edu

Prerequisites: None

Description
From the earliest games played with sticks and pebbles through today's virtual worlds and ARGs, students will be exposed to video game design and development, and will create concept documents for games of their own.

Format
This class is designed as a multiplayer game.

Class time will be divided between fighting monsters (Quizzes, Exams etc.), completing quests (Presentations of Games, Research etc.) and crafting (Personal Game Premises, Game Analysis Papers, Video Game Concept Document etc.).

At the beginning of the semester everyone in the class will choose and name their avatars. The first task is to craft the premise of a game you would like to design. This may be a board game, video game (AAA, casual etc.), massively multiplayer game, alternate reality game, or...? Guilds to craft these games will be chosen, balanced as closely as possible by 1337 skillz and interests. Guilds will choose their names, and group in their starting zones. Guild membership will be determined by final class size.

Each guild will be composed of one member from each of the following character classes:

Mage (Designer)
Ranger (Writer)
Warrior (Programmer)
Healer (Artist)
Necromancer (Producer)

It is not compulsory to be 1337 in any character class. For example not every guild may have a strong artist. Since the final assignment is a concept document, rather than a video game, buffs such as Internet Graphics may raise the player to the level necessary to succeed.

Grading Procedure
You will begin on the first day of class as a Level One avatar. Level Sixteen is the highest level you can achieve (**IN DEVELOPMENT**):

Level	XP*	Letter Grade
Level Sixteen	1860	A+
Level Fifteen	1800	A
Level Fourteen	1740	A-
Level Thirteen	1660	B+
Level Twelve	1600	B
Level Eleven	1540	B-
Level Ten	1460	C+
Level Nine	1400	C
Level Eight	1340	C-
Level Seven	1260	D+
Level Six	1200	D
Level Five	600	
Level Four	300	
Level Three	150	
Level Two	75	
Level One	0	F

*Your level will be determined by experience points (XP) on a 2000 XP scale. You gain XP by defeating mobs, completing quests and crafting.

- Solo: Craft your own game proposal. (Written, 1 paragraph to 1 page, 50 pts.)
- Solo: Present your game proposal to the class. (25 pts.)
- Solo: Sell your game proposal to the class. (**Extra credit**. 25 pts.)
- Raid: Guild reading presentation (75 base pts. each person, 1 of these per guild)

- Pick-Up Group: 2-Player reading presentation (150 base pts. each person, approx. 1 of 11 available, cannot team with fellow guild member) **OR**
- Solo: 1-Player reading presentation (150 base pts. but easier than above, 1 of 2 available)

- Developing clever strategies to defeat presentation mobs can increase XP gained by up to 100 additional pts. (See **Raid Strategies** Below)

- Guild: Exploration of new zones. (50 pts. total, including final Guild vs. Guild PvP)
- Solo: Craft short report on *Senet* (Written, 3 pages, 75 pts.)
- Solo: Craft short analysis on board game of your choice (Written, 3 pages, 100 pts.)
- Solo: Craft analysis on video game of your choice (Written, 3 pages, 125 pts.)

- Solo: Defeat Five Random Mobs (5 reading quizzes, 250 pts. total)
- Guild: Midterm Prep Guild vs. Guild PvP (50 pts.)
- Solo: Defeat Level Boss (Midterm Exam, 200 pts.)
- Guild: Paper Prototype (50 pts. each)
- Guild: Defeat Final Bosses (150 pts. See **Final Bosses** below)
- Guild: Craft Final Project: Game Concept (Written, 30 pages, 250 pts.)
- Solo: Class attendance (280 XP total, 10 pts. per day of attendance)
- **Extra credit** for early completion of final concept document (10 pts. on Monday)
- Solo Farming: Glossary (**Extra credit**. 1 pt. per term added. 25 pt. cap per player. First come first served. Each mob only spawns once.)
- Group: Peer Review Secret Ballot (**Extra credit**. 0-100 possible XP as follows:
  - Guild Leader 100 pts.
  - Raid Leader 75 pts.
  - Solid Guild Crafter 50 pts.
  - Needs Rez 25 pts.
  - Leroy Jenkins 0 pts.

Grading is rigorous. Spelling, grammar and punctuation must be proofed. Total XP will suffer otherwise.

Expansion Packs

This game is currently in closed beta, so a number of changes may occur throughout the semester. The development team is working on the following for future expansion packs. For example:

- LMS class website. The site will mature and expand throughout the semester.
- Leaderboards will be added and published online. However, we must juggle hardcore competition with privacy, so in a university setting this is harder than it sounds.
- You will notice that as currently established the XP system is atypical with an equal number of XP required to reach each level. This results in the opposite of a normal MMO leveling curve: leveling up in the beginning is currently actually harder than at the end of the semester.

Raid Strategies

As noted above clever raid strategies can increase the amount of XP awarded for defeating presentation mobs. As in any MMO successful raids are built upon the attempts of others. Your basic slideshow presentation where you read off the bullet points like some tired professor will only qualify for the base number of XP. Other methods such as videos, contests, performances and of course games are encouraged.

Final Bosses

Late in the game guilds will be faced with two or more Final Bosses, game industry professionals, each harder than a Lich King. They will be required to defeat these bosses by selling them on their game concepts. Bosses this semester are Jesse Schell and Chris Foster. You can find their stats online.

Attendance and Conduct

Attendance will be taken, and will count toward the final grade (see above). You are expected to attend every class. Assignments are due at the *beginning* of every class. Late assignments will fail to achieve the highest amount of XP for that assignment.

Plagiarism, submitting assignments written by others, and other forms of academic misconduct are governed by university policy. In a word: DON'T.

Classroom conduct: Participate with civility and an abiding appreciation for the power of words. Respect others, even those who hold opposing views.

Required Text
The Art of Game Design. Jesse Schell.

Suggested Reading

Homo Ludens. Johan Huizinga.
Flow: The Psychology of Optimal Experience. Mihaly Csikszentmihalyi.
A Theory of Fun. Raph Koster.
Game Design (Second Edition). Bob Bates.
Game Design: A Practical Approach. Paul Schuytema.
Rules of Play. Zimmerman & Salen.
Understanding Video Games. Egenfeldt-Nielsen et al.
Character Development & Storytelling for Games (Second Edition). Lee Sheldon.

Figure 7.1
Fall 2010 syllabus.

A new addition to the format section was an attempt to map more gamer references on to real world elements. It had always felt artificial to create avatars and guilds, and then refer to the roles that players would take on by real-world professions. So in this iteration, I settled on fantasy role-playing classes instead.

Designers became *Mages* because there is a good deal of magic in the initial creative process that gives birth to an idea that can grow into a game, a movie, or a symphony.

Writers became *Rangers*. I was on shakier ground here! I am a writer, and I play rangers or their equivalents (hunters, archers) in almost every role-playing game I play. One of the reasons I chose fantasy role-playing classes is because I like fantasy better than other genres, such as science fiction, horror, dystopia, and so on. Some small self-justification can be found in Richard Bartle's analysis of player personality types in MMOs, as shown in Figure 7.2.

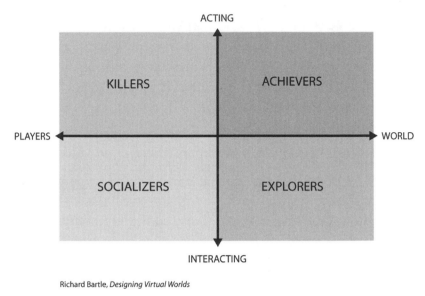

Richard Bartle, *Designing Virtual Worlds*

Figure 7.2
Richard Bartle's four player personality types.

There is no need to go into great detail here. Bartle's book, *Designing Virtual Worlds*, examines the four major player types and their relationships to a virtual world and other players. Simply put, they are the following:

- **Killers.** These players would rather fight than talk. They prefer PvP to PvE. This is not, as some suggest, a negative category. It is one of the primary homes of those who play for the competition.

- **Achievers.** Achievers play for extrinsic rewards, such as levels and loot. They can be equally strong competitors.

- **Socializers.** Their enjoyment springs from interacting with other players. The game matters less than the social experience.

- **Explorers.** Explorers play to discover new things; to go where others have not yet gone; and to lead the way for others through maps or hints.

Few players of MMOs are entirely one type. However, we can often be identified primarily by one type. I am an explorer. Writers are *explorers*—leading the way, finding new paths.

Bartle's personality types are good for more than justifying my role-playing class for writers. We will be going into game design in greater depth starting on Level 11. But it's worth mentioning here that your class is divided into these four types as surely as any MMO. When you design your game, it would be folly not to include equal gameplay for each of them.

Programmers became *warriors*. They are usually in the thick of battle, and if they fail, the battle is often lost. Without programmers, there is no video game.

Artists became *healers*. As Congreve wrote in his play, *The Mourning Bride*: "Music hath charms to soothe the savage breast." (Yes, it's "breast" not "beast.") Art has long been known to heal by changing attitude, and therefore physiology, by reducing stress and fostering relaxation.

No, they aren't perfect. I am still struggling to make the student's avatar relevant in a game design class, not just consistent with the world of the game I'm designing. As we will see on Level 9, in that class, the solution is far simpler.

Under the "Format" heading of the syllabus I also went into more detail about how students, even freshmen, could fulfill the various roles they would be asked to play in the design of their guild's game. For this, I introduced another game concept: buffs.

Buff

> A buff is an enhancement to a player's power, either permanent or temporary. A permanent enhancement is bestowed by the game mechanics, such as leveling. A temporary enhancement is caused by something within the world of the game, such as a spell.

In this case, I wanted to reassure students that they need not be experts in the role in which they ended up. Remember some may not have gotten their first or even second choice. It would be difficult to force someone without programming experience to be responsible for making programming choices even if they weren't required to code. Pointing out to them they could research into what their role required, or rely on examples and images they didn't produce themselves, was sufficient to soothe a number of savage breasts.

The next big change was the table under "Grading Procedure." I wanted to try and tackle the imbalance in the leveling I described earlier. I was careful to add the words *In Development* because this didn't feel right either. I added additional lower levels, easier to reach with less XP. However, the glaring error was that with the first five levels, the only thing achieved was the level itself. It was little consolation to someone who was gaining XP and levels relatively fast, only to see online, where their grades were tracked, that they still officially had an F.

My last class session every semester is a "postmortem," a term the game development community has borrowed from a medical examiner picking apart a corpse to determine how the victim died. In the industry, it is the game that is picked apart, features discussed, design decisions studied, and personnel issues scrutinized.

My classes are the victims that the students get to pick apart on the last day. We have an open dialogue about what they felt worked and what went wrong. And more often than not, their observations help me make my next class better. Nothing was dissected more thoroughly in the first three classes' "postmortems" than the leveling system. Thanks to the students, I think in the fourth iteration (still ongoing at this writing) we'll discuss in Level 9, we're finally getting close.

Despite the lack of interest in glossary building the previous spring, I again trotted this out as a worthwhile exercise to gain some extra XP.

BRAND NEW PARTS TO THE SYLLABUS

Following the "Grading Procedure" section, I added three new parts to the syllabus. The first of these was "Expansion Packs."

Expansion Pack

In development after the initial release of a game, expansion packs add new material, including additional story, new areas to explore, new items, and sometimes more levels.

Here I explained the two major challenges I had identified. One was the leveling system. The second was Rensselaer Learning Management System (LMS). This was the promise that I, the game designer and developer, would continue to work on these items in the hopes of correcting them as the semester wore on. I failed with the leveling system.

Using LMS was a mixed bag. It is an adaptation of the *Blackboard Learning System*, a course administration tool used by a number of universities. At

Indiana University, we had a similar system called *Oncourse*, which, in turn, was an adaptation of a competing system called *Sakai*. These well-meaning tools all feel cobbled together by any number of programmers who are not educators and educators who are not programmers. They can be in almost the same breath helpful and time-saving and frustrating and time-wasting.

Luckily, I had the help of an LMS guru by the name of Marie-Pierre Huguet, then Instructional Designer at Rensselaer, and her team of talented students. Marie-Pierre had introduced LMS to my orientation class before my first semester started. It seemed more flexible than Oncourse, particularly in the graphical look-and-feel of a course. Oncourse looked like a course administration tool. In LMS, we created a map of a fantasy role-playing village for the class with seven icons representing buildings and other features of the village (see Figure 7.3).

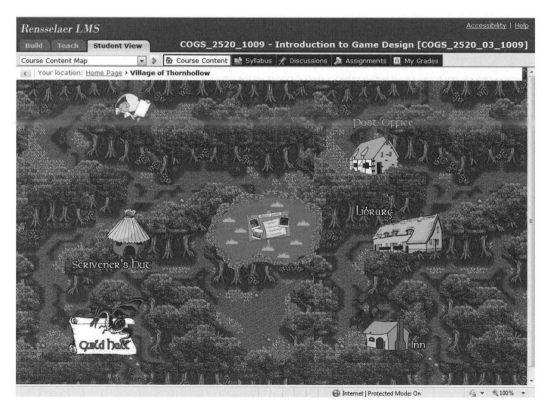

Figure 7.3
LMS village map of the "Introduction to Game Design Multiplayer Classroom."

Each of the seven icons was meant to be a link to course content. Rolling over the icon displayed a tool-tip naming the *icon*. Clockwise from the upper left-hand corner, they are as follows:

- **Town Crier.** Clicking on the Town Crier would take students to the LMS Orientation website. Here they could learn where to find the syllabus and calendar; how to check their status in the class; where to upload assignments; and so on.

- **Post Office.** The Post Office would link to a page where they could find class assignments.

- **Library.** Here students could browse through the syllabus, calendar, and click on links to outside content such as other RPI resources and Internet articles pertaining to game design issues.

- **Inn.** This was planned to be a forum for students to contact one another and discuss class issues.

- **Guild Hall.** All six guilds had rooms here where they would communicate privately; find photographs of themselves and their avatar names; and later in the semester, a brand new surprise courtesy of one of our Final Bosses. This will be revealed on Level 8.

- **Scrivener's Hut.** This was a link to a wiki where students could upload glossary items.

- **Notice Board.** Announcements of important class events would be posted here.

In addition to these features for students, LMS also allowed for the recording and posting of grades, a drop box for assignments, and other tools for building the website and administering the class. We were stretching LMS to its limits. We'll see on Level 8 how all of this worked out.

The next new section in the syllabus was called "Raid Strategies." Here, for the first time, I laid out in black-and-white what I expected from the presentations, a rubric that had been only verbal in the previous classes.

Finally, there was a section called "Final Bosses." With this class, industry guests became a more formal part of the class. Guild presentations to guests pretending to be publishers would now be graded. As you can see in the syllabus, the guild pitches of their concepts, were worth a good chunk of XP. While points were based on the first draft of the concept documents, and not on students' ability to pitch their ideas, guest comments were directed at everything. Our two Final Bosses were Jesse Schell, professor at Carnegie-Mellon's Entertainment Technology Center and CEO of Schell Games (and, as you will remember, the guy that gave the talk that led to this book), and Chris Foster, Design Director at Harmonix and Lead Designer for *Beatles: Rock Band*. This was a great success, and a Q&A panel with our guests later that afternoon was standing room only. As of this writing, a video of the wide-ranging session can be found at *www.hass.rpi.edu/pl/hass-events/games-speakers-jesse-schell-chris-foster*.

So, while maintaining the format of previous multiplayer classrooms, I explored a number of new ideas for "Introduction to Game Design." Let's go up to Level 8, and you will see how they turned out.

Here are the real-world terms in this chapter that map directly to game terms.

Table 7.1 Terminology Map

Designer	Mage
Writer	Ranger
Programmer	Warrior
Artist	Healer
Student Aid	Buff
Ongoing Class-related Issues Being Addressed	Expansion Packs
Hints on Improving Presentations	Raid Strategies
Industry Guests	Final Bosses

LEVEL 8

INTRODUCTION TO GAME DESIGN CLASS

Rensselaer Polytechnic Institute sits on a hill overlooking Troy, New York, and the Hudson River Valley, as shown in Figure 8.1. On the far side of the river to the southwest is Albany, the state capital.

There are a number of differences between Rensselaer and Indiana University. Rensselaer is a private university with approximately 7,500 students on its 275-acre Troy campus and a satellite campus in Hartford, Connecticut. Indiana University, Bloomington, a public university, and the flagship campus in the Indiana University system on over 1933 acres, had over 42,000 enrolled students in 2010.

Rensselaer, founded in 1824, is the oldest technology-based university in the English-speaking world, and retains a strong focus on its technological roots, especially engineering. Coincidentally, classes were first offered at IU in 1824. IU's roots lie in the liberal arts and sciences. It was officially designated the "State Seminary," and its first secular president was not elected until 1883. In 1945, it became the home of the Kinsey Institute for sexual research.

IU's mission remains one of providing higher education to primarily Indiana residents. Although 68% of students were from the state in 2010, 49 other states and the District of Columbia are also represented, as are 165 foreign nations. Rensselaer consistently ranks in the top 50 universities worldwide for technology, and among the top 50 universities in the United States for overall academics.

Figure 8.1
Rensselaer Polytechnic Institute.

As of this writing, IU does not offer an undergraduate video game degree. However, the Department of Telecommunications offers a sequence of related courses in Telecommunications devoted to Games and Interactive Media from which students can create a major. Area Certificates in Game Studies and New Media and Interactive Storytelling are offered to non-Telecom students. And IU has an Independent Major program where students, working with faculty mentors, can craft their own personal majors in many fields, including video games.

Rensselaer has its interdisciplinary Games and Simulation Arts and Sciences (GSAS) program, which offers multiple majors, minors, and dual degrees in all facets of video games with concentrations in fields such as Arts, Human Computer Interaction, Computer Science, Management/Entrepreneurship, Cognitive Science, and Physics.

Each approach reflects its institution's history and mission. IU's program grew from its strong liberal arts tradition. Rensselaer's program clearly reflects its science and technology roots.

While all of my students are of the gamer generation, the above facts go a long way toward explaining the differences between the two institutions and how the multiplayer classroom was affected when I moved from one institution to the other.

- **Class size shrunk from 30–40 students to 25.** Guild size shrank from 6–7 members to 4. Presentation quests required more material to be covered by each player.

- **Class time grew from an hour and fifteen minutes to an hour and fifty minutes, and it was now worth four credits instead of three.** I was afraid I wouldn't have enough material to fill the additional 35 minutes! For the first couple of classes, this proved correct. But while at IU, I often had to push material from one class to the next when quest presentations went long. I discovered that the extra 35 minutes eliminated that need, and the class stayed much closer to my original calendar.

- **There is another result of longer classes for four credits.** It means there are fewer classes available to students. Rensselaer requires a certain number of classes for a student's major. If they choose to pursue a dual major, corresponding courses are required. And there is yet another group of institute-required courses in both math and science and the humanities and social sciences. This restricts the number of classes that students can take in their chosen major, and I believe restricts our ability to give them all the knowledge we could to prepare them for their careers in any segment of the video game industry.

  This is a balancing act many schools face, and it goes back to my earlier comments on Level 7 concerning the tug of war in academia between those who research and those who make. A curriculum becomes an uneasy compromise between the two that pleases no one completely.

- **Students at IU entered with a wide range of interests and goals.** Some were interested in careers in the game industry; others were casually interested in games; still others knew little about games, but wanted to learn more. Coursework had to reflect that wide range of interests. A good question to ask to gauge the level of interest in games was "Who was Leeroy Jenkins?" About half of my "Theory and Practice of Game Design" class knew.

- **Students in GSAS arrive focused on careers in video games, whether commercial or applied.** In the entire "Introduction to Game Design" class, all but one or two freshmen, knew who he was, and debated whether the video of his exploits was real or staged.

- **Some students at IU could draw from a wide range of skills necessary to the production of video games.** Others had none. This meant I could not ask each guild in a class of juniors—no matter how balanced I tried to make them—to build a playable portion of a game at the end of the semester.

- **All students at RPI entered the GSAS program with high math and science scores, as well as skills such as programming and art and writing already developing.** These students were on a much more equal level of knowledge even as freshmen coming in. This, in turn, meant that guild balancing was simpler, and I did not need to tailor class content to the same wide range of abilities as I had at IU.

Another difference was the addition of Marie-Pierre Huguet and her team, who documented the class with video. The stills on this level, and on Level 10, have been grabbed from Flip video, shot by several people, including yours truly. The quality reflects the videographer holding the camera at the time.

Other differences will become apparent as we study how the "Introduction to Game Design" class played out. First, take a look at the new game board.

Here we have an entirely different classroom arrangement: square tables each designed to accommodate four students, and each anchored in place by cables from the floor leading to electrical outlets on the tables for laptops (see Figure 8.2). Every incoming freshman is required to have a laptop.

This room shared the advantage that the Ballantine classroom enjoyed: easy to divide the guilds. Each table was an easily identifiable zone. However, the flexibility ended there since the tables could not be moved more than a few inches from the power cables.

Since 25 students had enrolled in the class, it made sense to divide them into five equal-sized guilds of five players each. The main issue here was that the tables were only designed for four students each. Seating five at a table was a bit cramped, but we made do, as shown in Figure 8.3.

Figure 8.2
Sage Laboratory room 2510.

Figure 8.3
The guilds in their zones.

ZONES

Since we were back to video games instead of the subset of multiplayer games, I changed three of the zone names.

- **Mount Miyamoto.** Named for Shigeru Miyamoto, Japanese video game designer and producer at Nintendo who has created some of the most successful video game franchises ever, including *Mario*, *Donkey Kong* and *The Legend of Zelda*. He is the first person to be inducted into the Academy of Interactive Arts and Sciences' Hall of Fame.

- **Isle of Wright.** Will Wright returns from the previous game, the creative force behind the Sims franchise.

- **Caverns of Bartle.** As the co-creator of the first MUD, Richard Bartle also returns, representing multiplayer games.

- **Romero's Ruins.** John Romero, the co-founder of id Software, is responsible for popularizing first-person shooters with the classics *Wolfenstein 3D*, *Doom,* and *Quake.*

- **Sid's Swamp.** Sid Meir is the designer of *Civilization*, widely considered to be one of the best video games ever created. He is the second person to be inducted into the Academy of Interactive Arts and Sciences' Hall of Fame.

They were arranged like this in Figure 8.4.

Again guilds were moved from zone to zone. I used this chart to track guild movement throughout the semester.

A more formalized procedure was adopted for players answering questions about the people their zones were named after. This culminated in December with another PvP event where guilds were required to defend or reject, including these designers on the game map. They did not know which zone they would end up in the day of the competition, so they were required to research all five. All guilds chose to defend the inclusion of the zone's namesake. The debate started slowly, but picked up rapidly with members of other guilds challenging their conclusions. After the defenses, everyone voted on who had done the best job.

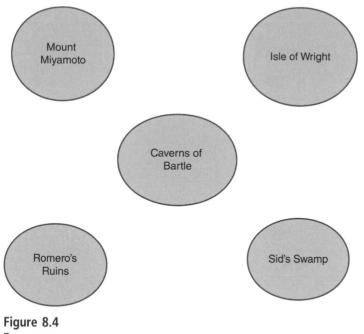

Figure 8.4
Zone map.

We began as before with everyone making up their avatar names. I asked them to bring physical representations of their avatars. I'd tried this in the "Multi-player Game Design" class, hoping it would help me remember student names as guilds moved around the classroom. But it was still more difficult without a fixed seating chart. The "Introduction to Game Design" class was no better at bringing their avatar pictures and models, but this was in part due to the fact they were much more elaborate. So an additional idea of making the avatars more prominent went unfulfilled. Happily, this issue easily resolved itself in the "Designing Interactive Characters" class that we'll visit next.

Here are the avatar names in Table 8.1 and their fantasy role-playing classes. See Level 7 for how these classes map to real-world jobs on a game development team.

Next came the game pitches. Five games were selected for which students would create their concept documents. The guilds were created as before, juggling player choices with balanced skill sets (see Figure 8.5).

Table 8.1 Avatars and Classes

Avatar	Class
TACO_reaper	Warrior
Globemeister	Necromancer
Taiyokami	Healer
The Iron Chef	Ranger
Chiminee	Healer
B422	Healer
Favian	Mage
Atlas	Ranger
Nero	Healer
NoRaptors	Necromancer
RamenNoodles	Mage
HowOriginal	Ranger
Espada6	Warrior
Legendman	Necromancer
Edrobot	Ranger
Acro Star	Warrior
Spaceman Sam	Mage
IOOl	Warrior
Filipino Spartan	Warrior
SirDrBodkin	Ranger
Sinister Duke	Necromancer
Ketsueki Ten	Mage
Trex	Mage
Rosalita Maria	Healer
Hat Guy	Necromancer

Here are the guild names that players picked and the games that each guild would design, as shown in Table 8.2.

I confess to a prejudice against the small group of genres AAA titles tend to fall into: Survival Horror, Post-Apocalyptic, Post-Tolkien Fantasy, and Science Fiction. Happily, casual games and some AAA titles widen the field, but when I look at *The King's Speech* nominated for 12 Academy Awards this year and *Black Swan*, another independent film that is enjoying a great box office, and notice that the demographics of video games is widening radically, I can only hope the publishers of AAA titles will be more willing to widen their horizons.

Figure 8.5
Announcing the guilds.

Table 8.2 Guilds and Games

Guild	Game
Bloodbath & Beyond	Infiltration
Neo Arcadia	Hallowhunt
Mystery Box	Super American Presidents
TBA	Brush Paint!
Triple Rainbow Inc.	City Survivor

So I haven't been surprised when there were many pitches in all of my game classes for games within the few genres mentioned previously. We did manage to have two Post-Apocalyptic games in this mix, but each with some interesting elements. We also had a great Halloween game, a parody of first-person shooters where you could play a butt-kicking American president, and an art-based game where your avatar defeated evil beavers by painting in "all the colors of the rainbow." All in all, an interesting group of games!

I noticed something almost immediately that was the same at both IU and RPI. Class attendance was outstanding. In fact, it was no longer necessary to pass around a paper for those present to sign. I could take attendance by looking at the classroom. On only one day when several students were attending a conference did I have more than one person absent. Total absences for the entire semester were 10. Of those, only two did not inform me in advance that they would not be able to attend. Out of 700 possible absences (25 students × 28 class stations), there were only 10 absences—including the winter. In upstate New York. In neck-deep snow.

I believe there are two reasons for this. The first is the nature of the multiplayer classroom. Students do not know what to expect, either from the instructor or their peers. They had a great time learning, as the photographs in this chapter will confirm. The second is the simple flip from telling them they would be graded down, if they missed a class, to telling them they would get XP just for attending. What a simple change. What a gratifying result!

Crafting began again with *Senet*. Other crafted reports were on an analog game (board game, card game, etc.) of the player's choice and a digital (video) game. Players brought in analog games they had reported on for the rest of the class to play.

Finally, quest presentations took on a life of their own. During the postmortem last spring, my "Game Design" students had suggested I not only suggest avoidance of bulleted PowerPoints, but I give some examples of successful presentations. I used their class as an example, mentioning the *So You Want to Be a Millionaire?* game, the scripted performance, and more. This semester's class took those examples to heart.

Quest presentations featured lots of audience participation; several games; mods of several video games from *Super Mario* to *Subversion*; a website that could supposedly identify a real or fictional person from a few scant clues (it failed to identify the Game Master of this book, however...); examples within the wonderful award-winning *Minecraft*; an expert demonstration of close-up magic; and an original epic poem.

Mod

Mod is short for modification. It means an experience that is not stand-alone software, but built from the assets and programming of another game. Today many commercial games include the ability to easily create mods.

Minecraft

Minecraft is a highly entertaining "sandbox fantasy adventure game" set in a world made of different kinds of one-meter blocks that players can manipulate in all sorts of interesting ways.

The best part of these presentations was not their considerable ingenuity, but their clarity. The presenters did not lose touch with the fact that they were sharing knowledge. And thanks to the entertainment, not in spite of it, the lesson was learned (see Figures 8.6–8.9).

For random mob attacks (the reading quizzes), I reverted to solo written exams, but added a twist. This idea was inspired by a comment from one of the contributors on the Gaming the Classroom forum. Aaron Pavao, a Math and Computer Science teacher at Waunakee Community High School in Waunakee, Wisconsin, described a way that players could contribute to their guild's success:

> "[I] implemented a "teamwork bonus" system wherein if all of the members of a team do well on an individual test, they get an XP bonus. This leverages social pressure to encourage students to encourage one another to prepare."

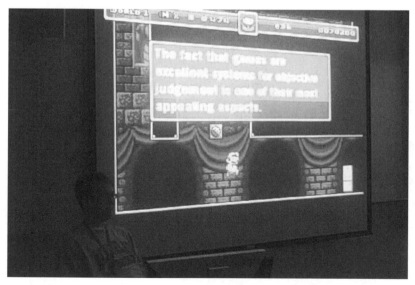

Figure 8.6
Edrobot enlists Mario's aid to teach game design.

Figure 8.7
Mindcraft is the setting for Bloodbath & Beyond's quest presentation.

Figure 8.8
Favian uses card tricks to illustrate his quest presentation.

Figure 8.9
HowOriginal begins his presentation: "To not bore people with traditional PowerPoints, let us test the strength of words."

Allowing guilds to answer one question for all to succeed in the first two MCs had two drawbacks. As mentioned earlier, it encouraged laziness in a guild. If only one member studied, in the end, those who didn't bother would suffer either on the midterm, or in their ability to contribute to the concept document. Second, it placed a lot of weight on a single question. If the entire guild knew the answers to all of the questions on the quiz, except the one the random roll of a die chose for them, they would fail to get *any* points on that quiz.

So this time, while they were individually taking the quiz, if *any* guild member got the bonus question correct, all got credit for it. Here was another intrinsic reward: doing something to help guild mates.

I had learned the previous semester how important it could be to engage everyone in preparing to attack the level boss (midterm exam). I kept the guild vs. guild PvP that had worked so well the previous semester at IU but added a physical element.

Differentiating who shouted out a word or zone name first proved difficult, and it caused a great deal of passionate debate. I tested another approach in

"Introduction to Game Design," introducing the Hat of Knowledge, a baseball cap courtesy of one of my IU colleagues, Edward Castronova's Ludium conferences.

I placed the cap on a table at the front of the class. Each guild selected a representative to line up along the wall. I randomly chose 1 of 60 questions, of which 40 would be on the midterm.

Instead of shouting out answers, each of these pullers waited for a signal from their guild and then raced for the hat (see Figure 8.10). The first one to grab it had a few seconds to hear the answer from his guild. He would then officially answer it.

Puller

> In MMOs, a puller is a member of a group or raid who is tasked with pulling a mob to his comrades, usually so it will not aggro other nearby mobs. This technique is important when a group is able to kill one mob but could not handle more.

Some would jump the gun, grab the hat, and wait in vain for their guild to give them the correct answer, as shown in Figure 8.11.

Others had better success, as Figure 8.12 clearly illustrates.

Figure 8.10
Guild pullers prepare to attack.

Figure 8.11
Sorry, Atlas, looks like your guildies left you twisting in the wind.

Figure 8.12
Mystery Box scores!

As before, the amount of XP the class earned on the midterm was significantly higher than the non-MC classes. Although I'm truly sorry we don't have a shot of RamenNoodles plummeting over the table in his attempt to grab the hat, I'm even happier that the multiplayer classroom failed to sustain its first injury!

THE PROTOTYPE

An important stage in the development of a game is the prototype. This can be a level, or a quest, or some other portion of the game that demonstrates significant gameplay. Developers blessed with a good budget, a reasonable schedule, technical expertise, and hopefully a stable engine can build a prototype that can look and feel much like the finished game. Publishers usually include this as a milestone in the contract with the developers.

In none of the first three multiplayer classrooms did we have that luxury, but that's okay. Long before the prototype publishers demand, developers often create what is called a *paper prototype*. This prototype may be built with other materials. They may even be digital, as shown in Figure 8.13. But its primary purpose is to test gameplay as early in the production cycle as possible. This we could do.

Figure 8.13
TBA's prototype of *Brush Paint!* was digital but with a human player-character.

Figure 8.14
Spaceman Sam explains the intricate rules to *City Survivor* to testers.

First, as we did in previous classes, rules for the games were posted online in advance of the prototype session, so that playtime would not be wasted with explanations of rule sets (see Figure 8.14). However, as in previous classes, not all that many players bothered to read the rules in advance. This shouldn't be surprising to game publishers who a number of years ago stopped including more than the most rudimentary manuals with their games. Players don't want to read rules. They want to play!

Luckily, being gamers, they picked up the games very quickly on the day. One member from each guild stayed at their table to game master their prototype. The other guild members moved from table to table, playing each game for a set period of time.

After feedback from their testers both during play, and in a postmortem session in the next class, guilds polished their game concepts. Their hardest test yet was quickly approaching. On November 19, they pitched their games to the Final Bosses: Chris Foster and Jesse Schell, as shown in Figure 8.15. Chris and Jesse played commercial game industry publishers: cold, heartless beasts who could wipe guild raids in a few seconds.

Actually, both of the Final Bosses were tough but fair: grilling guilds on their designs, budgets, assumptions of how the commercial game industry operates, and much more (see Figure 8.16).

Figure 8.15
Neo Arcadia raids the Final Bosses with their game Hallowhunt.

Figure 8.16
Boss Mobs Jesse Schell (foreground) and Chris Foster on the attack!

Jesse's use of Livescribe's Echo pen allowed him to simultaneously record the pitches while he wrote his notes. I then uploaded links to each guild's house on LMS that allowed them to access files on Livescribe's website where they could read his notes as they simultaneously heard the recording of their pitch, giving a much clearer idea of the specific moments he was reacting to.

For the first two classes, average grades had risen from a C to a B. This time the average final grade leapt from a B to an A-. I'm pretty sure this wasn't due to the teaching method I employed. Nor do I think it was entirely due to the fact that RPI requires higher SAT scores than IU for admission. I confess I went a little crazy with this iteration of the multiplayer classroom, piling on several opportunities for extra credit that had not appeared in the syllabus simply because several games, including a variation on musical chairs, seemed like good ideas worth trying. I did this without using my less than l33t math skills to their fullest extent. As a result, the grades were skewed higher for just about every student. I promised myself I would be far more diligent with the next class.

And that next class we will look at in Levels 9 and 10, "Designing Interactive Characters," would prove to be a major departure from the structure of the first three. Even though it is still in progress, the significant changes make it worthwhile to include it in this book. And Level 11 will take us away from game design classes altogether to see how other teachers in other fields are designing coursework as games.

Observations from Marie-Pierre Huguet

Beyond the Game

This is the first day of class. I walk into the classroom with a wave of students. It is one of these rooms designed to facilitate cooperative learning. The rows of desks have been replaced by eight square tables. Each is surrounded by four, randomly arranged, neon green or fluorescent orange plastic chairs. Painful attempt at cheering up the grayness of everything else. The room is equipped with the high-tech paraphernalia of a wired institution: hubs at the center of the table, cutting edge technology at the faculty podium.

After careful selection, I settle in the back of the room and assume my role of observer. More students trickle in. They must be freshmen. They have the stiff air of their class. Pretending to know what they are doing by furtively getting their cues from those already settled. As they sit down, most open their laptops and start typing away. Those not on a laptop are on a cell phone, iPhone, or droid. They look like any other student on campus. At Rensselaer, regardless of your major, you're an engineer.

There are two doors. The one we all used, opposite the windows, by the teacher's podium, and the one almost hidden at the shadowy end of the class by the whiteboard. This is the one Lee chooses to enter the classroom. He's wearing a T-shirt and Bermuda shorts and is holding a handful of papers. At first, not everyone pays much attention to him. Though older, he could be one of them. Probably a staff member working on a degree of some sort. They're used to that. They type on. Some have struck up a whispered conversation with their neighbors. The class is starting soon, and you don't want to seem too rowdy on the first day.

Rather than join one of the groups, however, Lee stops by the long table in front of the classroom and stands there, looking around. A few students look up before dismissing him again. A TA, maybe? Not worth their attention either. Some are beginning to look concerned. Where's the professor? It's twelve noon. A younger man is accompanying Lee. They readjust their thinking. You can't have two TAs in a class of 25. I see puzzled looks. Aren't professors supposed to wear suits and ties on the first day of class? Carry laptops or some academic-looking things?

Slowly the students are beginning to pay attention to Lee. Very superficially at first. He introduces himself and his TA before launching into the syllabus. That's the familiar first day of the semester traditional routine. They've already been through a couple of these. They expect him to get into the grading stuff, the attendance and conduct policies, the no-late-assignment spiel . . . and they start drifting again. Not for long. "You all have an F, says Lee, unless . . ."

A lot can happen in a nano second. And a lot does happen between the moment the students hear "F" and "unless." In that infinitesimal amount of time, they come together as one against the injustice. I hear a few "What?" "Hey!" "Not fair." They are ready to stand up for their rights as students, argue this newcomer to the ground. But as Lee continues, barely raising his voice, yet reaching the back of the room, they realize they have entered "the game." Comprehension sinks in. Excitement rises. They're already plotting to be the first to get to Level 1.

Although multitasking resumes, the flying fingers on the keyboards have shifted purpose. Text a friend to urge him to get into this section of the course. Google "Lee Sheldon" to check on the non-assuming man standing in front of them. Brush up on gaming terminology . . . without appearing to be doing so. I catch "raid," "XP," "mob," and "1337 skillz." Personally, I would have fed the entire syllabus into these search engines. I am an educator, not a gamer.

And as an educator, I see beyond the game. This is the ultimate situated learning opportunity where the subject being taught is the vehicle used to teach it. It uses the language that needs to be spoken, the behavior that needs to be learned, the process that needs to be followed. It has the messiness of life, and the rigor of academia.

In this educational environment where the teacher has turned into a Game Master and the students hide behind avatars as they defeat mobs, complete quests, and craft games, the overarching shadow of academe looms forcefully. This remains a "real" course, with "real" learning outcomes, and "real" assessments. It is a critical component of Rensselaer's "Games and Simulation Arts and Sciences" program and as such is held at the same high academic standards as all other classes.

From my observer's perch, I am watching a familiar world. I may not know the lingua franca, get confused by the landscape, puzzle over the characters, but I recognize the driving forces behind it all. Piaget, Vygotsky, and Bruner walk side-by-side with Miyamoto, Wright, Bartle, Romero, Meir, and Schell.

Piaget is omnipresent in the environment Lee has created. Lee intuitively understands the critical role that experiences play in his students' learning. He is aware that they construct their own knowledge in response to these experiences. Given an opportunity, students will learn many things on their own without the intervention of peers or instructors. They are intrinsically motivated to learn and do not need a grade, or a "reward" from the instructor to motivate their learning. The true act of learning is, after all, a selfish, self-centric experience. The levels in the game, while measuring the specific accomplishment of predefined educational tasks, keep the control of reaching that level with the students. As the Game Master, Lee's role is to facilitate and orchestrate the learning, not to control it.

Though Lee might be hard-pressed to discuss the concept of "continuity," the key sources needed to establish this Piagetian concept are present. For example, the *reading presentations* allow his students to "translate incoming information" into a form they and their peers can understand (assimilation). When they select their avatar and become part of a guild, the students adapt their current knowledge structures in response to new experience (accommodation). And their *raid strategies* allow them to balance assimilation and accommodation to create stable understanding of game design (equilibration).

Vygotsky provides the framework that structures the interactions between Lee and his students. For most of the semester, as the Game Master, Lee is the "more knowledgeable other." He has designed his learning activities to enable his students to solve problems and perform tasks that would otherwise be hard or impossible for them to carry out. But he also shares that role of a more knowledgeable other with his students and his peers. This Vygotskian framework for learning is driven by the notion of the *zone of proximal development* or *ZPD*. ZPD characterizes the area between what the students can accomplish on their own and what they can accomplish, and ultimately master, with the help of a more knowledgeable other. The four critical learning stages of ZPD are omnipresent in Lee's class:

■ **Stage 1: Assistance provided by more knowledgeable others.**

In Lee's class, the students are never left alone to struggle with a concept, a task, or an assignment. At any time, they can turn to their guild, to the other guilds, and to the Game Master. And even as they reach their final "level," as they present their game concept, they receive guidance and feedback from external experts in the field: Jesse Schell and Chris Foster. A reinforcement that, though the "Introduction to Game Design" multiplayer game might seem to be over, the learning that came with it is not.

▪ Stage 2: Assistance by self.

The structure of the course allows the students to take ownership of their learning. The passive attitude so common in our classrooms disappears on the first day of class. "You all have an F, unless . . ." somehow is the most powerful trigger for student engagement. This is not about making the grade anymore. It is about getting to the next level, challenging oneself, alone or with others, outsmarting the Game Master. This may be a multiplayer game, but the careful blend and the nature of "solo" tasks allow the students to reap the most XP's on their own terms.

▪ Stage 3: Internalization.

In an introductory course, the assumption is that the students need to acquire the skills, knowledge, and attitude that will facilitate the successful completion of their course of study. In academia, this often means an overdose of theory anchored in behaviorist mechanics. The role of practice then is to support and reinforce the theory. Learning remains static and limited to the subject at hand. In the multiplayer classroom, the roles are reversed. Practice drives the understanding of theory. As the skills, knowledge, and attitude are acquired, students create their own schemas out of which, ultimately, theory will emerge.

Internalization allows the students to take a learning opportunity and make it their own. At this stage, they move away from the ZPD, and they build their understanding of the "what" and the "why," and strengthen their knowledge of the "how." As they experience the various aspects of game design by defeating mobs, completing quests, and crafting, they are exposed to the theory that hides behind each of them. Theory loses its abstraction and perceived staleness to provide the sound and critical structure needed for strong game design. Theory comes to life as students craft their game. Lee provides learning activities that foster student ownership of their knowledge, and this knowledge becomes meaningful to them.

▪ Stage 4: Recursiveness through prior stages.

Though the course progression seems to be linear, perception skewed by the "level" approach of the grading structure, it is not. And in many respects, neither is the students' progression through the four stages. Once the students have progressed out of the ZPD and have taken ownership of their knowledge, the learning does not stop or become static. Students remember concepts discovered on their own, yet there are still many instances when they need assistance while learning something new. This is facilitated by this stage of "recursiveness through prior stages," one of the driving forces in Lee's class.

In the syllabus as much as in the classroom, I can see how Lee introduces the students to the basics of game design through direct involvement and reflection, builds on them, before weaving in the complexity that requires mastery of the initial skill and knowledge sets. For example, the students play *Senet*, an assigned game that will enable them to write their first reflection. The feedback from this assignment can then be used when they write a short analysis on the board game they have selected before writing a full analysis on a video game of their choice.

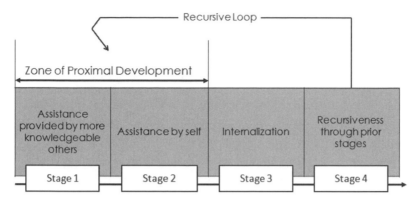

Figure 8.17
Recursiveness through prior stages.

With the first instance, the game of *Senet* has been selected for the students, and Lee's interaction with the groups of players is more overt. He walks around the classroom, guiding and refocusing the students as they play (stage 1). With the second instance, the students are taking Lee's role, becoming the more knowledgeable others. They have selected the game, and they are responsible for facilitating the activity (stage 2). Finally, the familiarity of playing the game is removed, and students focus on the skills of writing a game analysis (stage 3). Stage 4 is reached when students start working on the creation of their own game.

Figure 8.17, derived from work by Gallimore and Tharp (1990), provides a visual representation of the process.

Lee's gaming of the syllabus is a form of discovery learning, an inquiry-based, constructivist approach proposed by Jerome Bruner, that thrives on problem-solving situations: The students draw from their own experiences and knowledge to discover facts and relationships. They interact with the world, real or imaginary, by exploring and manipulating objects and situations, wrestling with questions and challenges, and performing tasks and experiments.

Here, the syllabus becomes more than a piece of paper with placatory words stamped onto it. As Bruner states in *The Process of Education*: "The first object of any act of learning, over and beyond the pleasure it may give, is that it should serve us in the future. Learning should not only take us somewhere; it should allow us later to go further more easily." Bruner argues that, in order to enable the transfer of thinking processes from one context to another, students need to learn the fundamental principles of a subject matter rather than just master the facts.

As Bruner suggests, Lee encourages his students to construct hypotheses, make decisions, and discover principles by themselves. He has organized his content, identified the skills required, and illustrated the theories to be learned in ways that allow his students to build their new knowledge on their existing experiences. Lee facilitates a recursive learning process that is strengthened by scaffolding. This powerful, constructivist approach results in students that are actively engaged, motivated, autonomous, responsible, and independent. Most of all, the tailored learning experience enables the development of their creativity and their acquisition of critical problem-solving skills. Ultimately, the students own their knowledge because they are so entwined with its construction.

In Lee's classroom, the students play an active role in their learning. . .and in Lee's. Learning has become a reciprocal experience for all. As much as Lee facilitates his students' learning of game design, they impact his understanding of what teaching is all about. Each iteration of the course, each rewriting of the syllabus, each rethinking of the game, challenges Lee's personal, epistemological stand. But this, dear reader, is another story.

So from my observer's perch, I continue to watch Lee's world of praxis and theoria as he creates unique learning experiences for his students, and they create amazing teaching opportunities for him.

REFERENCES

Bruner, J. (1966). *Toward a Theory of Instruction*. Cambridge, MA: Harvard University Press.

Bruner, J. (1960). *The Process of Education*. Cambridge, MA: Harvard University Press.

Bruner, J. S. (1967). *On Knowing: Essays for the Left Hand*. Cambridge, MA: Harvard University Press.

Vygotsky, L. S. (1978). *Mind in Society: The Development of the Higher Psychological Processes* (A. Kozulin, Trans.). Cambridge, MA: Harvard University Press.

Piaget's theory. In P. Mussen (ed) (1983). *Handbook of Child Psychology*, Vol. 1. New York: Wiley.

Flavell, J. (1996, July). Piaget's legacy. *Psychological Science*, 7(4), 200–203.

Jean Piaget (1950). *Introduction à l'épistémologie génétique*. 3 Vols. Paris: Presses Universitaires de France.

Gallimore, R. & Tharp, R. (1990) Teaching mind in society: teaching, schooling, and literate discourse, in: L. C. Moll (Ed.) *Vygotsky and education* (Cambridge Cambridge University Press), 175–205.

LEVEL 8 STUDENT EVALUATION QUOTES

"Not going through the whole survey. Great class. The game style of the class was fantastic. Felt a little disorganized at a few points though, but overall a great class."

"The structure of the classroom rocks."

"I enjoyed getting a different experience here than any other course I have taken. What made it so different was working in the same team for the entire course; none of my other group projects have been "long term." While I did learn a great deal from the lectures and book, I enjoyed being able to learn about working in a team the most. I do feel a bit uneasy since we didn't cover how to make many different types of games, like the other game design class, though."

"Professor Sheldon's unique method of teaching the course paid off very well. I felt like I learned a great deal that I wouldn't have otherwise, had Professor Sheldon not taught the class."

"I really enjoyed Professor Sheldon's class. I learned a lot, and I appreciate the time that I spent in the class. He also helped me determine whether or not to continue in this field, and it was highly useful. Thanks Professor. :)"

Case History 3

Louisiana State University: Introduction to the Study of Education

Jessica Broussard, PhD

Department of Curriculum & Instruction

College of Education

Louisiana State University

Remember the definitions of stereotypical hard-core and casual gamers on Level 7? Some gamers don't even realize they *are* gamers, as Professor Broussard discovered when she polled her class in this case history. She also discovered that educators being trained with traditional methods may get uncomfortable when faced with alien concepts like creating avatars and leveling up.

As we will see, though, this didn't discourage her. Her own familiarity with *World of Warcraft* and console games helped her come up with the idea of rewarding them with achievements. Regular rewards are a prime design component of video games, so they fit perfectly into the multiplayer classroom. And Professor Broussard was able to successfully tie achievements back into XP.

Professor Broussard (see Figure CH3.1) also noticed a number of changes in the social interactions in her class as time went along.

Figure CH3.1
Jessica Broussard.

The course formally titled "Introduction to the Study of Education (Intro to Ed)" was designed with the beginning pre-service teacher in mind. The course description in the class schedule read for prekindergarten through third grade only; however, this did not deter a handful of students from other majors from finding their way onto the roster.

The gamed version of this course had been taught over two semesters at a large southern university. Almost all of the students in "Intro to Ed" were 18–21-year-old white females. Over two semesters, only three males had registered for the class, and of those, only one actually wanted to become an educator of any sort. Most of the students were second or even third generations of their families who had attended college; some were the third generation who had become teachers at this particular university.

The classroom for the first semester was not small so much as filled with six large tables that were awkwardly arranged into the shape of Pi. They were placed this way to encourage group work. Yet this placement also prohibited movement around the room, making monitoring progress on classwork or handing out papers to individuals difficult and making the classroom seem very small. The room was equipped with a digital projector, connected computer, and document projector. These were placed in the front corner of the room farthest away from the door.

The classroom for the second semester was large enough to fit well over 60 students in its current design of seven long and often shifting rows. There was also ample space at the head of the classroom, which came equipped with a whiteboard, projector screen, and a technology lectern that allowed its user to use the document projects, desktop PC, and microphone. When fully occupied, moving around either classroom was difficult, to say the least, as was rearranging the furniture. So other types of activities could be equally difficult.

All students were comfortable with technology. The majority of students in each class had iPhones or other versions of smart phones. Generally, half the class brought laptops to the weekly face-to-face class. And many of those students had Facebook or some instant messaging program up during lectures or group work.

Even knowing how comfortable the students were with technology, at the beginning of each semester when I asked if any of the students were gamers, or would even consider themselves to be close to being gamers, not one hand was raised. I then asked about different types of games. Did they play *WoW* or *Call of Duty*, *Madden,* and so on, but still there was absolute silence, except on the faces of males who later admitted to wanting to claim their gamer identity, but already felt out of place being the only males in the room. They did not want the "nerd" stereotype that occasionally goes with the title of gamer to further separate them from the rest of the class.

It was not until I started naming the more casual games like *Farmville* or the *Wii Sports* that the female students became aware of the fact that they actually did play videogames, very regularly, bordering on constantly. To many female students, the understanding of what a videogame was could be most simply summarized as involving violence and a console. *Gamers*, in their minds were dedicated to or focused on a particular game or type of game, bordering on obsession. For these students, if the player could take a break and did not have to kill anyone, it was not a videogame, and if they did not possess a certain level of interest, they were not gamers.

I introduced the nature of the course by changing the language of the standard syllabus. My students did not participate in weekly assignments; instead, they had quests (presentation of chapter materials). In-class assignments generally were referred to as mini-quests or side quests (depending on the size or import of the assignment.) The biggest assignments were the raids, which in other courses were called *practicum* or *field work,* and the final boss, or final exam. Even though this exam had to take the form of a traditional multiple choice, students took the exam as guilds.

Most of the students were completely unaware of or inexperienced with the MMORPG genre and felt uncomfortable with the idea of creating an avatar and even the overall language, at first. Because of their particular definition of game and lack of experience, certain concessions were made so that they would be able to more comfortably approach the teaching methodology. I removed the ideas of creating avatars and leveling up. Many of my students did not see starting off as a level one avatar and building up from there as the development or evolution of character, but as more of a punishment, as if they had already failed. They were more comfortable with the idea of starting off the class with a clean slate and seeing each grade as a success.

This need for success is also where the greatest innovation for my version of the course came from. My students wanted to be able to see their successes and with my own experiences with WoW and Xbox, I developed the idea to give them achievements.

Weekly, students had the opportunity to earn several achievements based on their online quest work for the week, forum discussion participation, and reflective blogs. Students were only required to post an initial response to the forum discussion and respond to two others—three total. Any number of students could earn these as long as they contributed substantive posts.

- **Shine:** for posting 4–6 comments
- **Super Shine:** for posting 7–9 comments
- **Mega Shine:** for posting 10 + comments a week

Other achievements were based on the content of their posts and were far more subjective, usually only one of each was given.

- **High 5:** This was for a comment that struck me as deserving of congratulations (earning a good grade, overcoming a personal, academic, or professional hurdle, or coming to an unexpected and meaningful conclusion).
- **Hmm:** This was for a comment that they believed as a student but could change as they became teachers.
- **Golden Apple:** For mentioning their raid/practicum experience.
- **Good Sport:** For being able to not take my devil's advocate comments personally.

- **Backbone:** For commenting on something they saw in class that struck them as inappropriate.
- **Eddie:** For the best performance in a blog.

Each week's class started with the PowerPoint or Prezi presentation that announced the winners of each award. Students who earned the second type of achievement had the opportunity to discuss what they had written, which would lead into a whole-class discussion. Often, this was the student's opportunity to bring up topics that were not in the realm of the week's presentation subject, but that they were still curious or concerned about.

The results of this interaction and feedback were successful, but not as much as they should have been, based on how I had witnessed gamers react when they got certain achievements. At first, students were not excited about earning them, so they did not strive to do so. I asked about this later in a focus group, and it came out that there was not enough of an incentive for the students to do the extra work, especially for the higher level Shine achievements.

Right before the midterm of the first session of the course, I made the announcement that achievements would be converted into XP for the final grade point calculation. Essentially, according to the number of achievements they earned, I would add a percentage of that number of points to their final grade. Once this sank in, students could be seen counting the number of times they had been awarded an achievement. (PowerPoints and Prezis were available for them to see on the class's online learning environment.)

Soon, students began to *metagame* the class. Those who usually did not remember to participate were earning Super Shines. Students who rarely had anything of reflective value in their blogs were starting to go back through to previous winners' blogs to see what they had discussed to emulate the posts. So while this may seem as if they were not getting the most out of the assignments, especially the blogs, I felt they were working with an exemplar and now could see what good reflection looks like. This also encouraged them to participate not just more often, but also more substantively than they did previously.

Having seen this trend in the student's behavior, I decided that for the second session of the course that I would make this announcement at the beginning of the semester, but that I would increase the number of achievements students would have to earn before extra XP/grade points would be given.

I believe that it was because of this incentive that the number of students earning the Shines (all levels) dramatically increased. In the first week of the first session, only three students out of 25 earned any level of Shine, approximately 8%. In the first week of the second session, 12 out of the 35 on the roster earned Shines (approximately 29%), while three earned Super Shines (approximately 8%), and two earned Mega Shines (approximately 6%). In all honesty, this was the week that I felt compelled to create the Mega Shine award as one of the recipients made 11 posts, and another 13, and I had never witnessed this level of participation in the course before.

At the end of the first session, I asked students why there was the sudden increase in people earning Shines and other achievements. My informant "S" said perhaps a little too honestly, "Well, they finally had a point."

While observing the students receiving the achievements, interesting social aspects of the class began appearing, namely the competitive nature of the female students. The young women started bickering among themselves about who should have earned an award. There were also rumors of me being biased and favoring certain students when giving awards. This is understandable, as I tended to be suspicious of those students who suddenly began reflecting on subjects that they previously never mentioned or when posts seemed to be disingenuous. As the *Game Master*, I did not want to feel like I too was being *metagamed*.

During the course debriefing or postmortem, I sought out the students' opinions about any additional changes they would like to see for the future with the method and about the methods in general.

The changes many wanted to see were more fair distribution of points per achievements and better uses of guilds. According to many students, they wanted to see the Super and Mega Shines be worth more than the Shine. The most often requested was that each Super should be worth two XP counts and the Mega three. They also wanted to see the Eddie be worth more than the other subjective achievements. He was often touted amongst the players as being the top honor each week, ostensibly because of the appearance of the slide (see Figure CH3.2).

Figure CH3.2
The Eddie.

The other main change that they wanted to see was to make other groups treat the students as guilds did when presenting. Students often presented the content materials and neglected to use the groups mainly because the physical space made it difficult for students to separate into individual groups. So more often than not, when a guild presented materials, the students were approached as individuals and given some form of worksheet/study guide or divided into halves or thirds when competing in games.

At the end of the course, I asked the students to submit anonymous statements about how they felt about any aspect of the course. Some complained about their specific guild or the topic they had to present or wished they had gotten more achievements. However, one student (I still do not know which) stated:

> I have never heard someone say, "This is your mission." This is the quest that you have to go on. It is an awesome idea to set up a class around a

game, because essentially when you are in college or in school, your quest is to get to the finish line: to get that A or to get that B that you want in that class and to achieve your goal, to learn whatever you are supposed to learn. This really intrigued and motivated me."

I simply do not believe that there could be a better advertisement written or reason for continuing to use and develop this method.

LEVEL 9

DESIGNING INTERACTIVE CHARACTERS SYLLABUS

The full name for this course is "Designing Interactive Characters for Digital Games." In the curriculum, it falls in the second semester of the Games and Simulation Arts & Sciences major. It is predominantly made up of sophomores with a handful of upperclassmen. Several students are not GSAS majors but are students in related programs such as Electronic Media Arts and Communication.

Even though as I write this we are still several weeks from the end of the semester, and observations are necessarily incomplete, I felt that because the course was significantly different from the first three multiplayer classrooms, giving the information I have on it to date, would prove helpful.

My dilemma was twofold: Once you teach any class as a game, your students have played that game. They know both the structure and the content. If they take a second class from you, or if their friends take the class you have taught already, they can game the class.

Game

Used as a verb, to *game* or *metagame* means to exploit the design of a game; to use that design in ways it was never intended to be used to beat the game.

CHEATING VERSUS HACKS

Many in the gamer generation have grown up believing cheats are a legitimate part of playing games. There is a subtle distinction to be made here. Most would never condone someone overtly cheating by using a hack in a game for an advantage over other players, any more than they would condone cheating at football or poker by breaking the rules.

Hack

> *Hack* has a number of definitions, not all of them negative. As Wikipedia states, it may refer to "a clever or quick fix to a computer program problem." But it may also refer to "a modification of a program or device to give the user access to features that were otherwise unavailable," and that, in turn, would give the player an unfair advantage over opponents.

The rule sets in video games are not often as clear as they are in chess. In fact, designers hide some rules deliberately to provide a more satisfyingly competitive experience.

The gamer generation has come to believe that some cheats are benign, if they give them an advantage in getting past particularly difficult challenges. These cheats may take the form of hints, walkthroughs, "Easter eggs," or hacks. They are so common in video game culture that developers routinely build them into games, and game websites and magazines feature them, usually explicitly calling them *cheats*.

Easter Egg

> An Easter egg is a hidden feature of a game. These may be as simple as a text message, or as elaborate as entire levels unlocked by a secret keystrokes.

Cheats, unlocked by cheat codes, entered via controller or keyboard, are benign because not everyone is a hard-core gamer with the l33t skills necessary to complete the game. Some players want to see the next step in a game story, and to avoid frustration, use cheats or a walkthrough to help them get past obstacles in order to continue the story.

Walkthrough

A walkthrough is a step-by-step guide to every obstacle, every puzzle, every boss in a video game—and how to triumph over them.

We who design multiplayer classrooms are already blurring lines between game and reality. We shouldn't be surprised if game-savvy, problem-solving players apply their skills to gaming our designs, if we allow it. And sometimes we should!

Good students in the very first multiplayer classroom, "Theory and Practice of Game Design," would figure out how much XP they needed to receive a grade they wanted. If they were doing well accumulating XP, they knew they could afford to miss a class and still have enough XP so that it wouldn't affect their grade. Since this only works for students who are already doing well in class, I have no problem with it. To me, this is in keeping with the benign cheats gamers are familiar with.

However, allowing students to gain an advantage over the game I designed and to therefore achieve a higher final grade, falls squarely into that other kind of malicious cheating. It would be the same as finding out test answers before the test. I was compelled to change those elements of each game that could be hacked, like reading quizzes and exams, so the new crop of students wouldn't be able to learn answers to questions from an earlier class.

The other issue, if students take a second or third class from me—and many will do so over the course of their studies—an entirely new type of game is required each time. To do less would be to duplicate the experience enough students have had already, similar to teachers who recycle the same tired syllabus over and over again.

A NEW SYLLABUS FOR A NEW GAME

Happily, "Designing Interactive Characters" has given me the opportunity to strike out into new territory, literally. I've taken lessons learned from designing alternate reality games that take place in an even larger swatch of the physical world than a classroom to move us out of that single room. Let's have a look at the syllabus in Figure 9.1.

1

Rensselaer Polytechnic Institute
Games and Simulation Arts and Sciences

75047& 75048: Designing Interactive Characters for Digital Games

Section COMM-4210-01 & 02
Spring 2010
Days and Times TF 12-1:50pm
Room 2510 Sage Laboratory

Instructor: Lee Sheldon
Office: 4403 Sage Laboratory
Phone: 276-8264
Office Hours: TF 11-12
Email: sheldc2@rpi.edu

Prerequisites: COGS-2520 or permission of instructor.

Objectives
- Provide you with a framework for analyzing and designing game characters.
- Improve your analytic and design skills (including process skills)
- Introduce you to the practices of writers and designers who create characters in the games industry and in other media.
- Improve your presentation skills
- Add a completed project to your design portfolio

Format
This class is designed as a fantasy multiplayer game. You are the players. You will each create an avatar that will represent you in the game.

All you know is that you have been summoned to represent your guild at a mysterious gathering at the tower of a mage a continent away. Why you were chosen and the reason behind the gathering is unknown. Over time you will discover it.

This is an extremely hazardous quest. You will travel in a small guild party, balanced as closely as possible by 1337 skillz and interests. Hopefully the avatars you choose will support and complement one another so that you can overcome the challenges you will face, both natural and unnatural (Quizzes, Character Analysis Papers, Presentations etc.). Luckily your avatars will gain new skillz as they level up. These skillz are awarded with **extra credit**, and may be applied to any assignment.

At the beginning of the semester everyone in the class will choose and name their avatar, and choose their avatar's profession. Your next task is to decide the name and nature of your guild: its purpose and the land where it makes its home. Guild membership will be determined by final class size. You will

2

begin your journey in your home territory, your starting zone. But your journey will take you outside of that territory, the classroom, and into the unknown reaches beyond.

It is not compulsory to be 1337 in any particular profession. The final project will be an effort of the entire class. As the semester goes along, and the ways of avatars are revealed, more time will be allotted to it.

Grading Procedure

You will begin on the first day of class as a Level One avatar. Level Twenty is the highest level you can achieve. Your class letter grade will be determined by your final level. **You must be at least Level Ten to pass this course**.

Level	Skillz	XP[1]
Level Twenty		1000
Level Nineteen		930
Level Eighteen		900
Level Seventeen	5	870
Level Sixteen		830
Level Fifteen		800
Level Fourteen	5	770
Level Thirteen		730
Level Twelve		700
Level Eleven		670
Level Ten	5	630
Level Nine		510
Level Eight		410
Level Seven		320
Level Six		240
Level Five	5	170
Level Four		110
Level Three		60
Level Two		20
Level One		0

[1]Your level will be determined by experience points (XP) on a 1000 XP scale. You gain XP by defeating mobs, solving puzzles and crafting.

- Solo: Create your level one avatar. (Written, 1 paragraph to 1 page, 15 pts.)
- Solo: Introduce your avatar to the class. (5 pts.)
- Solo: Create your avatar's 3 dimensions (Written, 1-2 pages, 20 pts.)
- Guild: present your avatars' 3 dimensions to the class. (5 pts.)
- Guild: Scouting: 5 observations of wildlife in its natural habitat throughout the journey. (50 pts. total)
- Raid: Guild reading presentation (50 base pts. each person, 1 of these per guild)

3

- Pick-Up Group: 2-Player reading presentation (75 base pts. each person, approx. Cannot team with fellow guild member) **OR**
- Solo: 1-Player reading presentation (75 base pts. but easier than above)
- Developing clever strategies to defeat presentation mobs can increase XP gained by up to 50 additional **extra credit** pts. (See **Raid Strategies** Below)
- Solo: Analysis of Real Person of your choice (Written, 3 pages, 50 pts.)
- Solo: Analysis of Analog Character of your choice (Written, 3 pages, 75 pts.)
- Solo: Analysis of Digital Character of your choice (Written, 3 pages, 100 pts.)
- Guild: Midterm Prep Guild vs. Guild PvP (25 pts.)
- Solo: Defeat Level Boss (Midterm Exam, 100 pts.)
- Solo: Final character stories (Written, 5 pages, 145 pts. each)
- Class: Craft Final Project: Create Mage's Chamber (Digital, 30 pages, 145 pts.)
- Solo: Class attendance (140 XP total, 5 pts. per day of attendance)
- Guild: Peer Review Secret Ballot (**Extra credit**. 0-50 possible XP as follows:
    - Guild Leader 50 pts.
    - Raid Leader 40 pts.
    - Solid Guild Crafter 30 pts.
    - Needs Rez 20 pts.
    - Leroy Jenkins 0 pts.

Grading is rigorous. Spelling, grammar and punctuation must be proofed. Total XP will suffer otherwise.

Hints

Information that may help you succeed in your quest:

- LMS class website. The site will evolve throughout the semester. Even though it will look like a map, it will be where you go to turn in assignments, check the class calendar, find additional resources and reading materials etc.
- Careful readers will notice that from Level 10 up the XP system mirrors percentages associated with letter grades.
- We will supplement the XP chart with a Leaderboard that indicates the number of students at each level to help track personal progress, particularly in the lower levels.

Raid Strategies
As noted above clever raid strategies can increase the amount of XP awarded for defeating presentation mobs. As in any MMO, successful raids are built upon the attempts of others. Your basic slideshow presentation where you read off the bullet points like some tired professor will only qualify for the base number of XP. Other methods such as videos, contests, performances and of course games are encouraged, even expected.

Attendance and Conduct
Attendance will be taken, and will count toward the final grade (see above). You are expected to attend every class. Assignments are due at the *beginning* of every class. Late assignments will fail to achieve the highest amount of XP for that assignment.

4

Plagiarism, submitting assignments written by others, and other forms of academic misconduct are governed by university policy. In a word: DON'T.

Classroom conduct: Participate with civility and an abiding appreciation for the power of words. Respect others, even those who hold opposing views.

Required Text
Character Development & Storytelling for Games (Second Printing). Lee Sheldon.

Suggested Reading

Better Game Characters by Design: A Psychological Approach. Katherine Isbister.

Calendar

The calendar will be found on LMS. It is subject to change; and will be updated. Check it regularly, especially if you miss class.

Figure 9.1
Spring 2011 syllabus.

You'll notice the section "Objectives" replaces "Description" from the previous courses. This course had been taught by several people before I inherited it. The bullet points were only slightly edited from previous syllabi.

The "Format" section introduces the new game. Not only would the class create avatars, but those avatars would also for the first time be instrumental to the game. Students would create detailed back stories for their avatars and choose specific professions for them. And these would be woven into the story of the game. Gone were the classes that represented game development team roles. These professions were part of their characters within the world of the game.

The movement from zone to zone would now represent that journey within the classroom. They would make this journey across a fantasy world that would also require them to move beyond the classroom into the unknown. I planned to make ARG-like puzzles that would send them out of the classroom, even out of the building.

Guilds would not only choose their names, but they would also each be given the name of their starting zone (a town in a land called *Valeria*) and a brief description of its primary feature. We will introduce these on Level 10. They would then bring their starting zone to life. No zones would be named after game design concepts or famous game designers. Again, these zones were located within the world of the game. I planned that together we would create a map of Valeria, indicating where the zones were in relation to one another, and I would suggest the direction their characters would travel to reach a tower of a mage who apparently was summoning them.

And because this was a class in creating characters, each guild would be given an NPC, again with a very brief description, that they would design together: name, physical description, past, current life, and psychology.

NPC

Unlike a player's avatar (or player-character) a non-player character (NPC) is controlled by the game program.

When we talk about three-dimensional characters, I don't mean characters modeled in software packages such as Maya or 3ds Max. I'm speaking of the three dimensions of character from drama.

Finding a precise definition of the term is a fascinating quest all its own. I take mine from *The Art of Dramatic Writing* by Lajos Egri. The three dimensions, according to Egri, are physiological (which I shortened to *physical* for my students), sociological, and psychological. I define them as follows:

- The physical dimension of a character is simply the physical description: height, weight, body type, ethnic origin, scars, deformities, and so on.

- The sociological dimension of a character is both past and present: the character's origin, upbringing, place of birth and so on, plus the character's current environment.

- The psychological dimension of a character is how the first two dimensions have formed the character's view of the world. Any two people born in the same place and with similar physical features may react entirely differently when confronted with conflict or a relationship.

The students would have two assignments to build characters, and those characters would change as the game developed. One of the concepts I teach in my game design classes is the "consistency" of the world. I tell my students that they can build the worlds of their games with any physical laws and rules they want, but everything within their worlds should follow those laws and rules. They should not be broken arbitrarily simply to provide a new gameplay obstacle or a twist in the story. Anachronisms are terribly hard on immersion.

To teach the students the concept of consistency, I allowed them a lot of freedom in their initial character designs deliberately so they might be forced to change them. Game design is not static. It is a process. We'll revisit these concepts on Level 13, when we go into more detail on how games are designed.

There were other significant differences to the format of the game. As in role-playing games, avatars would acquire new skills to help them in their quest. I hoped these skills would help to at last give me a reasonable leveling system, as we will see in a moment.

Finally, for the first time, instead of giving each guild a final concept document, the entire class would build a playable version of the final level of the game. At first, I envisioned this as the mage's chamber at the top of that mysterious tower, but when we had decided on how we would build the final level, and I realized the skill level of the class with programming and art was quite high, I decided to expand the assignment to include the entire tower with six doors that could only be opened by solving puzzles, and the grounds surrounding it dotted by magical fountains.

In the "Grading Procedure" section, I provided this class with a new version of the leveling chart. The changes were these:

- I dropped the explicit conversion to letter grades, although the admonition that students needed to reach Level 10 to pass the course was in bold type.

- There were 20 levels possible. This gave me a good range in which to distribute the total basic XP of 1,000 points.

- The first 10 levels closely resembled standard RPG game levels with increasing XP needed for each level.

- I added a new column. Again much like characters in standard RPG games, players would achieve new skills every few levels. At first I considered actual skills that would help them in their game quest.

This started to feel too elaborate. So instead I decided to cut way back on the random extra credit opportunities and give them 5 XP when they reached four levels to add to any grade they wanted. This I hoped would give them an additional incentive to do well.

Assignments underwent some changes, too. In addition to short presentations of their avatar names, they now first described them and then went into far more detail exploring the three dimensions of their characters. Originally, I hadn't planned to have the guilds create NPCs. However, between the time I wrote the syllabus and our first class meeting, I decided that experience creating an NPC was equally important, if not more important. It is a convenient method for game writers to bring emotion into their stories.

So the idea that each guild's quest would require them to escort an NPC with a certain disability to the tower was born. It was also then I began to toy with the idea of allowing their NPCs to die, if the guild fared badly on an assignment.

A new class of assignments was the "Scouting Expeditions." I originally planned for five but have now cut it to three. These "observations of wildlife in its natural habitat" would require the class, divided into guilds, to journey out into the real world to study real people.

When I kept quest presentations, I decided to drop the random mob reading quizzes for this class as an experiment. My thought was that the presentations would be enough to give them the foundations they needed to design their characters. I wasn't so sure, though, if they would be enough preparation for the midterm.

Instead of analyzing games, they would analyze a real person of their acquaintance (unconnected to the scouting expeditions), an analog character (from traditional media such as movies, TV, plays, books, and so on), and a digital character from a video game.

There would be no pitches to industry guests, and their final grade was divided into two assignments: the final digital project and a story featuring their avatars, and other student avatars and the NPCs they designed.

The "Hints" section featured another apologia for the LMS site. It's clear to me now that despite noble efforts on the part of a dedicated team, LMS has too many restrictions in its design to allow for the flexibility in graphics we hoped to achieve. While it handles grading and assignments well, I will have to look elsewhere for a format that can adjust to the unique elements of future multiplayer classrooms. Also included was a suggestion of how they could translate the levels they achieved to letter grades and the announcement of a first real attempt at a leaderboard, tracking only what levels had been reached by how many players.

The rest of the syllabus was relatively unchanged. The book under "Suggested Reading" was *Better Game Characters by Design: A Psychological Approach* by Katherine Isbister, the originator of the course, and it is recommended.

Now let's level up and see how the fourth iteration of the multiplayer classroom is faring this semester.

LEVEL 10

DESIGNING INTERACTIVE CHARACTERS CLASS

We have reached the last of the multiplayer classrooms I have designed to date. It's still ongoing, but already the quest across Valeria has produced some interesting results.

With all the changes in this syllabus from the first three, I wasn't quite sure what to expect. The most interesting one for me would be tying class events and grades to the narrative of a game. How would the players react to this shifting between fantasy world quests and real-world concerns?

I warned them early that because they were here to learn how to create characters, I would allow them to peek behind the curtain to see the Game Master at work. But I also wanted to see if an emotional attachment to their avatars and the NPCs they created could be nurtured and then utilized to create even more engagement in the class than I had seen before.

As we had in the previous game, in the first class meeting, I explained the concept of the multiplayer classroom and explained that the class would be videoed for research and for stills to be included in this book. Students signed releases and were asked to introduce their avatars in the next class.

From the very beginning, the many differences between this class and the previous classes were apparent. The first was that their avatars would inhabit a particular land called *Valeria*. And, repeating the setup from the syllabus, they were told that they would represent their guilds at a mysterious gathering at a tower on the other side of the continent. Why each is chosen, and the reason for the gathering is unknown. But it is promised that over time, they will discover the purpose of their quest.

USING BACK STORIES

A second difference was that before all that was required of students was to choose a name and a visual representation of their avatar, but here the assignment was also to provide a back story for them.

Back Story

The back story represents a character's life up until the moment the game begins.

Some simply read this back story aloud as themselves, ticking off facts. Many told their stories in character, as shown in Figures 10.1 and 10.2.

Figure 10.1
Albert, a bard, debuts his latest composition.

Figure 10.2
Dan, the jester, amuses his audience with a cartwheel.

Given that one of the lessons of the class is that the worlds we create in games should have an internal logic and consistency, no matter how foreign and fantastical they might seem, I deliberately gave them very little coaching about the land they were to inhabit. And since the lesson and the game are one, my intent was that over time their characters would evolve to more fully match the world.

This has already begun to happen. Back stories are shifting, sometimes subtly, sometimes dramatically to match the fiction of Valeria, as more and more of it is revealed to the players. Two touchstones that I expect to change, but have not yet changed, are a couple of character names and two or three guild names.

DESIGN CONSISTENCY

Remember that in previous classes this consistency was not demanded. Here, however, the class had a fictional setting that students would not only play within, but that they would help create. Also, given the name of the land and other suggestive words such as "mage" and "tower" for example, they had hints as to the setting of the game. This was not to be a multiplayer version of *Grand Theft Auto*. We were headed for that realm of high fantasy belonging to J.R.R. Tolkien and *Dungeons & Dragons*. So, not surprisingly, far more chose names for their avatars that might fit within such a game. Their avatar names are shown in Table 10.1. One student switched his avatar name from his original choice.

Table 10.1 Avatar Names	
Ving Maltir	Shrike
Dan	Reed Valcon
Korvin	Ra
Jerious	Sizara
Arryn Daker	Sagan
Clementine Xai (formerly known as Mr. DeLackey)	Fenris
	Firewall
Albert	Krin
Marcus	Menelek
Zalathrax	Kenna
Anath	Hipster
Kinigit	Thay

Notice how few of these role-playing names are entirely anachronistic, especially compared to earlier classes.

HOME SWEET HOME

Table 10.1 illustrates two more differences in this class. Gone are the guild concept documents. The final project is being shared by the entire class. Instead, players were introduced to six zones. They were told the names of these zones and given a very brief description of each:

- **Wadi Shir** was a small outpost built up around an oasis in a southern desert.

- **Scaleport** was a busy port city at the intersection of two rivers.

- **Fenwick** was a seaport in marshlands.

- **High Reach** was a sparsely inhabited mountainous region.
- **Miscato** was a town amidst a great forest.
- **Far Plains** were grasslands dotted with small settlements.

They were then asked to vote on which they would call their home. There were 23 students in the class. After some discussion, we ended up with five zones housing four avatars each and one, Scaleport, with only three. The seating was adjusted so that each who had chosen a particular zone was now seated with the others who had chosen it. These became the guilds, and they were asked to name them. The percentage of guilds with names consistent with the world we were creating was not as high as avatar names:

- Park Rangers
- Chasers of the Dawn
- Angry Fashion Crusaders
- Deathbone
- Aesir

And, after their Game Master rejected their first name as highly unsuitable for a university setting or for this book, the unfortunately named guild of three from Scaleport settled on Shady Goobers.

THE GEOGRAPHY OF VALERIA

We then discussed the geography of Valeria. In addition to the first presentation quests undertaken (a pick-up group and a guild quest), the crafting assignment for the following class was for each guild to produce a map of their home and describe something of the culture to be found there. With these in hand, each guild sketched a rough map of the land of Valeria and presented it, as shown in Figure 10.3.

The Game Master added mountains to the west with a pass to regions unknown. It was assumed, correctly, that the mysterious tower would be found there. Discussion in the following class resulted in the specifications for the final map (see Figure 10.4).

Figure 10.3
The guild Aesir presents its map.

This map was the basis for the LMS page for this class. Blackboard, the underlying software divides everything into tables of cells, and, as mentioned, is really not designed for the freeform graphics we wanted. This screenshot in Figure 10.5 is an early example of what we hoped would be an interactive map of the game world. It is a work in progress.

Tooltips inform students what the links are for each zone, except the Rift, the pass through the mountains into unknown lands. Clockwise beginning with the Rift:

- The Rift link is not yet activated.
- High Reach houses the syllabus and calendar.
- Fenwick is the assignment dropbox.
- Scaleport links to class announcements.
- Wadi Shir links to the LMS orientation.
- Far Plains is a window to outside resources.
- Guild halls are located in Miscato.

Valeria

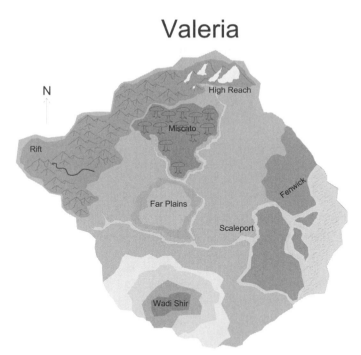

Figure 10.4
Map of Valeria by Hipster and friends.

Figure 10.5
LMS interactive version of the Valeria map.

The class follows a narrative. In many video games, there are two parts to good storytelling: the original writing and how the story is delivered to players. A major mechanism in this class is messages from out of nowhere. Are they from a mage in the tower that will be the quest's last destination? An opponent perhaps? At present, the source remains unknown. But these messages are delivered to the class in the form of PowerPoint slides.

MESSAGES FROM THE UNKNOWN

There have been four messages to date. For the first two, the entire class was able to see all six messages directed to individual guilds to foreshadow their involvement in the game's central quest (see Figure 10.6).

The text reads:

> "Inhabitants of the Wadi Shir
>
> There is one among you who must journey to a tower lost from memory

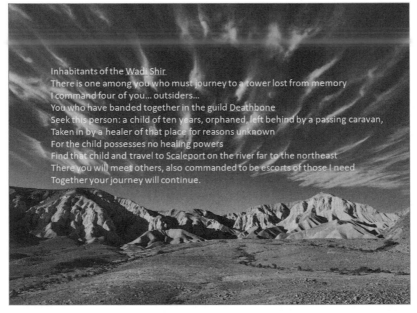

Figure 10.6
First message for the guild Deathbone.

I command four of you... outsiders...

You who have banded together in the guild Deathbone

Seek this person: a child of ten years, orphaned, left behind by a passing caravan,

Taken in by a healer of that place for reasons unknown

For the child possesses no healing powers

Find that child and travel to Scaleport on the river far to the northeast

There you will meet others, also commanded to be escorts of those I need

Together your journey will continue."

The text incorporates elements of the back story devised by the guilds for themselves and their home regions. And it introduces the next major element of instruction. As discussed on Level 9, each guild was tasked with building another character, an NPC for whom they would be responsible on the quest.

CREATING CHARACTERS

Most gamers are familiar with creating their own avatars. However, only those few in the class who were interested in becoming writers of video games had ever created a character in a story before. They were creating this character from the bare bones of the summons, giving the three dimensions of character, a back story, and a life. Plus, because each of the NPCs were flawed in some way, having lost a power that they once possessed, a power that had *defined* them, the students' stake in their NPCs would be increased.

The six NPCs, named by the students, were:

- Janus, a 10-year-old boy, who had healing powers, but had lost them. He would be escorted from Wadi Shir to Scaleport by Deathbone.

- Deri, a formerly prosperous seller of potions in Scaleport, now fallen on hard times. His potions had lost their efficacy for reasons unknown. He would be escorted from Scaleport by the Shady Goobers.

- Tom Foolery, a remarkable thief able to charm any lock to open or cloud the minds of victims to become almost invisible, whose skill had now vanished. He would be in the care of the Angry Fashion Crusaders guild in Fenwick.

- Jurmund Njordr, a hunter and tracker, who can no longer read the land he once knew or command the wild creatures to do his bidding, now under the protection of Aesir in High Reach.

- Medea, an ancient crone, once a powerful witch, whose spells now fizzle and die, accompanied in Miscato by the guild Park Rangers.

- Asha, a woman, once a shape-changer, but who had lost that power, protected by the Far Plains guild, Chasers of the Dawn.

The second message summoned all guilds to Scaleport for what was to be their first scouting expedition not only in Scaleport, but in the real world as well.

Stalking

To stalk is to follow or observe (a person) persistently, especially out of obsession or derangement. That's one definition. Here's another one: observing fellow human beings for the express purpose of learning about human characters from the source.

That second definition is what we were up to on a cold day in February when the class split up into guilds and spread out across campus to observe, take notes, and then report, as shown in Figure 10.7.

The text reads:

"Park Rangers, leave behind the forest

And travel southeast to Scaleport

There must you examine the good (and not so good) folk of that town

Study their ways.

The knowledge you gain may help you aid the ancient one called Medea

Then return home

Travelers will soon approach to seek you out

Be ready for soon your true quest will begin…"

Figure 10.7
The Park Rangers guild of Miscato is summoned.

The last slide, shown in Figure 10.8, carried more explicit instructions from the mysterious voice.

I had originally planned to have all guilds converge on a single dining hall, the Commons. But when it turned out that a number of them did not have dining passes, some went there; others went to the student union; and the rest braved the cold outside.

They had already analyzed a real person of their choice for a crafting assignment. So they had an idea of what to expect. Still, working as guilds brought out more insights as they discussed their observations and theorized on who the people were: their jobs, attitudes on life, what their relationships might be, and so on. Some observations reported in the discussion that followed the scouting expedition were superficial, but others were surprisingly deep for such inexperienced stalkers. Sherlock Holmes would have been proud.

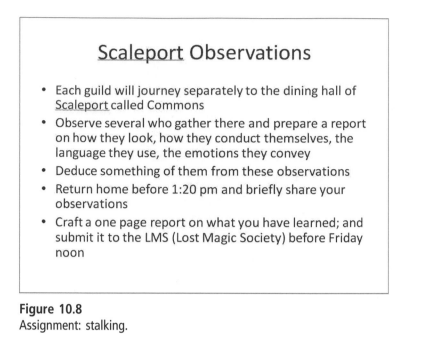

Figure 10.8
Assignment: stalking.

PREPARATION FOR THE FINAL PROJECT

Paralleling all of this main quest activity were two other activities. One was preparation for the final project, which was to create the final level of the main quest where all secrets would be revealed. We had chosen the *Neverwinter Nights 2* game builder tool for this. This is a relatively simple platform for game development, requiring some programming and little original art since it is intended to create mods of the *Neverwinter Nights 2* game, and that is also part of the J.R.R. Tolkien/*Dungeons & Dragons* universe. I have no doubt they could have produced several small games requiring more programming and art using their current skill sets. But I suggested this tool because I wanted to focus their attention on content, even more specifically on character design, rather than programming and 3D modeling.

The final project exists almost entirely outside of the game narrative because it involves building the level that completed the game. Students know, for example, that the final level consists of the tower and surrounding grounds; that there are six fountains on the grounds, but that they are not currently working; and that there are six doors that must be unlocked by solving puzzles using the lost skill sets of the six NPCS.

Teams, separate from guild affiliation, have been established:

- Programming, responsible for implementing gameplay, using a scripting language. Scripting languages are meant to be used with an existing programming language and are much simpler than programming from scratch.

- Art, responsible for ensuring that all players' avatars and NPCs are represented in the final level.

- Writing, responsible for the NPC dialogue.

- Audio, responsible for sound effects and music.

- Production, two producers responsible for seeing that milestones are met, as well as logistics, such as facilitating teams getting together, and so on.

On March 8, the team leads reported on goals for the Alpha stage of the final project. The Alpha was due on April 5.

Alpha

> *Alpha* is the phase in software development where testing begins and features are frozen, meaning that no new features will be added to the game. This is followed by *Beta*, where all features are completely implemented, and the focus is on usability testing and bug fixing. The final phase is *Golden Master,* when the software is ready to be released to consumers.

There were issues in getting the Alpha presentation up and running, but once it was, there was the tower surrounded by a field with six fountains leading to the door. All floors were implemented with placeholders until the Game Master could answer questions about the style in which they should be furnished.

PRESENTATION QUESTS

The second ongoing activity was the presentation quests on subjects such as 3D characters (defined on Level 9), character progression, pivotal characters, stereotypes, and so on. As the central quest progressed, these presentation quests prepared players for crafting assignments, such as the analyses of characters both real and unreal, as well as for the midterm boss battle.

Figure 10.9
Angry Fashion Crusaders challenge other guilds.

In Figure 10.9, we see the guild Angry Fashion Crusaders in the midst of their presentation quest. They illustrated key topics of their assigned material, such as challenging other guilds to add them to stories they made up on the fly. Candy was the extrinsic reward. Knowledge and practice were the intrinsic rewards.

ANOTHER MESSAGE FROM THE UNKNOWN

The third communication written on the wind was delivered differently from the first two. The means was still PowerPoint slides, but the messages were private for each guild. All players put their heads down on their desks. When a particular guild's slide was projected, members of that guild alone could raise their heads to read and record the message.

In the main quest, three of the guilds were now together in Fenwick: Deathbone, the Shady Goobers, and the Angry Fashion Crusaders. After everyone had seen their private messages, these three guilds were permitted to share their secrets with one another. The other three guilds were not present in Fenwick. Yet, they too, were given private information. Here is the message shown in Figure 10.10 received by Aesir, the guild still in High Reach.

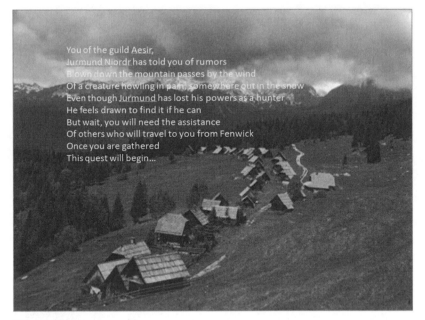

Figure 10.10
A message for Aesir.

The message for Aesir text reads:

> "You of the guild Aesir,
>
> Jurmund Njordr has told you of rumors
>
> Blown down the mountain passes by the wind
>
> Of a creature howling in pain, somewhere out in the snow
>
> Even though Jurmund has lost his powers as a hunter
>
> He feels drawn to find it if he can
>
> But wait, you will need the assistance
>
> Of others who will travel to you from Fenwick
>
> Once you are gathered
>
> This quest will begin. . ."

Then all were told that, while individual success or failure would be measured, the side quest referred to in their messages would be directly affected by their guild performances in the boss raid (midterm exam). They were assured that no matter what information was known by whom, this would not affect their ability to conquer the boss. But it was reiterated that how they did in the boss raid would be directly tied to the resolution of the quest and any phat l00t that might be rewarded for its completion.

phat l00t

phat 100 is more l33t speak. This refers to good rewards recovered after defeating a mob.

By this point, over halfway through the semester, solo and pick-up groups' quests, guild quests, the midterm prep PvP, the midterm boss raid, and crafting a digital character analysis have all been completed. Crafting final character stories, Beta (April 29), and the Golden Master (May 3) are all still in the future.

Quest Chain

Quests need not all be isolated from one another. Quest chains are a series of quests, one leading to the next. Quest suites are a group of quests related in some way, such as a single quest giver or geography.

Midterm Prep PvP

The "Designing Interactive Characters" midterm prep guild vs. guild competition was two weeks ago (early April 2011). One thing I changed in response to previous student comments was that, as can be seen in the syllabus on Level 9, we tallied points to determine winners, but those points did not translate to XP. This time I added some XP to sweeten the competition. The students had felt that it was a lot of work for no reward. There was, in fact, a mystery prize (flash drives) that the winning guild received on the last day of the semester. But there was no immediately obvious extrinsic reward. I felt the intrinsic reward, doing well on the exam, should have been enough. But I wanted to try adding a small amount of XP this time:

1st Place: 25 XP per guild member

2nd Place: 20 XP per guild member

3rd Place: 15 XP per guild member

4th Place: 10 XP per guild member

5th Place: 5 points per guild member

6th Place: Raid wiped (0 points)

Adding XP had no effect on the level of competition. It was still high, as you can see in Figure 10.11.

Figure 10.11
Intense competition, but lots of laughter, in the midterm prep.

However, after it was over, one student complained that the physical element of the competition was out of place in what was meant to be an intellectual exercise. He pointed out that the mentally agile players were at a disadvantage when facing more physically fit players. It wasn't just prep for an exam. His XP was at stake! I didn't want to lose the heat of the competition, which the physical task of racing for the Hat of Knowledge introduced, and the XP total wasn't large, but his complaint had some validity. In fact, I wanted to address it.

The problem, as I saw it, lay in the order of events. As before, each guild nominated a puller who would race other pullers to the Hat of Knowledge. The idea was that the winning puller would wait for his guild to find the answer in the book and then run for the hat. From there, they had 30 seconds to prompt him with the answer, which he then needed to repeat (sneaky memory trick as a game rule).

But the competition was so intense that pullers would grab the Hat of Knowledge before other guild members had found the answer, hoping that the answer ritual could be completed correctly in the allotted time. The only penalty for this was that if the guild failed to answer the question in time, they could not try a second time. The remaining guilds would race for the hat again, and since their guilds already knew the question, they had much more time to find the correct answer.

In addition to adding XP for this guild vs. guild competition, I added a new rule that was designed to address exactly what the student would ultimately complain about. Since I was adding XP, I wanted to try a two-tiered point system to focus attention on the intellectual, rather than the physical. The puller would have a chance to try and answer the question on her own before her guild could find the answer. But she would only get one point for it. If she waited, and grabbed the hat only after her guild signaled her they had the answer, and they indeed answered the question correctly, the guild would get two points.

Explaining this idea led to so much confusion, however, that I finally asked the class if they wanted to try it, or should I simplify the rules. They overwhelmingly voted for the latter. Allowing them to vote on the change in rules meant only the one student complained after it was all over. Not bad, but in the future, if this mini-game remains the same, I will try subtracting game points from the tally, whether they translate to XP or not, for wrong answers. That should shift the gameplay from "grab and hope" to "learn and then grab."

Midterm Boss Mob (Frost Lizard)

There were 50 questions on the midterm. And 40 of them were to be answered individually. For the last 10 as long as one member of a guild had the correct answer, all got credit. The satisfaction of helping the other members of the guild was the intrinsic reward.

At the top of the midterm was an introductory paragraph that one might not usually expect to see on an exam:

Midterm Boss Mob: Frost Lizard

Over 40 feet in length, the frost lizard is the largest and most vicious reptile known, and its bite is one of the most poisonous. To treat the victim of a frost lizard, you must create a healing poultice with which to dress the wound. One of the primary ingredients in this poultice is the blood of the specific frost lizard that inflicted the wound. So, defeating the creature and collecting as much of its blood as possible, is the only way to save its victim. Each adventurer will have the opportunity today to collect up to 50 drops of frost lizard blood. You will receive one XP for every drop of blood you obtain. Good luck. It won't give up its blood without a struggle. You may find you must shed some of your own. And there will be consequences if you fail. . ..

I totaled the XP each of the guilds received on the test. That number became the number of drops of blood needed to revive the victim of its attack: the creature howling in pain, as described in Figure 10.10. But that number also needed to be above a certain threshold or the creature, a snow leopard, would die no matter how valiant the efforts of the players.

That threshold was a C average for the class. Grades on the midterm were the highest of any exam I have ever given. The lowest grade was a B-. The average grade for the class was significantly higher. The snow leopard could be saved.

All guilds had taken the exam and therefore fought the frost lizard. Four were physically present. The guilds from Miscato and Far Plains participated as spirits. Once the exam had been graded, there was another series of messages from the unknown.

THE MOST RECENT MESSAGES

Four messages were very similar. They made it clear that the wounded snow leopard was to be transported to Miscato to Medea, the witch the guild Park Rangers were protecting. So five of the six guilds were united in Miscato. Each of their charges seemed necessary to saving the snow leopard, even though all had apparently still not recovered their powers. And each NPC had grown strangely secretive. Once in Miscato, they were faced with a choice: give all the blood they had recovered from the frost lizard to Medea, or retain it. Figure 10.12 is an example of one of the messages.

Figure 10.12
Message from the unknown for the guild Angry Fashion Crusaders.

The message for the Angry Fashion Crusaders text reads:

"Angry Fashion Crusaders,

You have braved the journey to Miscato despite your reservations,

Following Tom Foolery, the thief you have grown to trust

Despite his sudden passion for sly winks and insincere smiles

The witch spoken of by Deri is here

Under the protection of a guild of Park Rangers

The witch, Medea by name, demands the blood you have collected.

After she has gathered all the blood, she will try her spell

Although she has known only failure of late,

And then the child, now sickly himself, must call upon powers

That have deserted him.

So that the snow leopard may be whole once more...

But you must ask yourselves, do the others not see the snow leopard

Is a ravening beast? Once healed, who knows where its hungry eyes might turn?

Will you give Medea the blood?"

The messages concerning the snow leopard were neutral for Deathbone, the Shady Goobers, and Aesir. The message for the Park Rangers made it clear that they were to argue in favor of giving the blood to their charge, Medea. As you can see above, the Angry Fashion Crusaders were by far the most suspicious.

My intention was that the students would frame the debate from the points of view of both of the two roles they were given: players in the game and designers of the game. I felt sure they would be able to step outside the story and arrive at the decision that best served the game. The lesson, already articulated several times already in class, was that however much they might want the game they were working on to go, the needs of the game must come first. But I had made a serious mistake.

These were gamers, seasoned role-players adept at immersing themselves in a narrative, even one as thin as this one. They carried on an increasingly lively debate, but only taking positions consistent with their avatars' characters. I had allowed for the possibility that some guild or guilds might withhold the blood by creating two continuations of the quest. But I had to prompt the exercise to include their opinions as designers. And even then, one guild, Shady Goobers, was adamant that they had no idea which direction was more dramatic. Withholding the blood made for some great drama as the debate proved.

I had also kept them in the dark as to the plight Chasers of the Dawn were facing. All alone in Far Plains, they had their own issue: Asha, the shape-shifter they were protecting, had vanished before the battle with the frost lizard. They had been given the choice to search for her, or to remain in their village as they had been commanded. They chose to remain. On this day, the choice was offered to them again. Again, they chose to remain.

I realized too late that I had been caught up in maintaining the mystery of my story and had totally dropped the ball in terms of sharing the intentions of the Game Master. The debate should have always been from the point of view of designers, not characters. I should have made that clear.

In the end, I had Chasers of the Dawn members, as designers, relate Asha's disappearance. It took only seconds for several students to realize the snow leopard might in fact be Asha, who had somehow managed to shift into a snow leopard but was now for some reason trapped in that form. Still the Shady Goobers insisted, quite rightly as I've realized, they would not give up their blood. So the quest took the second path I had prepared, just in case.

I have resolved to learn from this mistake. The designers will have all but one final twist laid out for them. It was my intention all along to reveal almost everything long before we reached Beta. At first, the lesson I took away from this mistake was to reveal the mystery sooner. Actually, what I now realize, is that it is far better to "spoil" the surprises, so your team knows what is expected, particularly since they must build the final level! Sigh.

Otherwise, the semester is progressing well. Attendance is at its usual high (except for the Friday before spring break!), and I'm getting excellent enthusiasm and work from the students. My primary interest was how tying exam results to the narrative track would work. The good news is that the exam and narrative fit, but the debate lesson I had intended teaching, being able to separate personal wishes from what would be best for the characters and the game, became instead a lesson for me. And because their grades were so high, the death of an NPC would not occur.

My experiment was to see what would happen if an NPC died as a result of a low grade, meaning how would the students react? Or would their concern for the NPC's safety—a great way to evoke emotion from players in a video game— cause students to strive for higher scores? They did too well on the exam. So the answers must remain for another story.

There are a lot of clues and suggestions on how to create multiplayer classrooms in the previous levels and case histories. Now we will explore the development process so that any teacher can design a multiplayer classroom of his or her own.

CASE HISTORY 4

VALENCIA COMMUNITY COLLEGE: UNITED STATES HISTORY TO 1877

Carl E. Creasman Jr.

Professor of History

Chair of History Program, East Campus

Valencia Community College

Mixed results can be as instructive as outright success and failure. I include this case history as a demonstration of that. The observations by students are informative. The questions Professor Creasman raises about class design and how to measure success when comparing a classroom with elements designed as a game with a traditional classroom format are enlightening.

There was a small, but measurable increase in student learning as measured by classroom assessment techniques. And possibly the most heartening result is that Professor Creasman is determined to build on what he has learned and try again (see Figure CH4.1).

I have been playing games since the mid-1970s when, as a pre-teen, my father taught me to play chess. As my love for history grew, I drifted to historical re-creations of actual events from the U.S. Civil War and World War II. When personal computers emerged in the late '70s, my best friend (and most avid gaming partner) and I broke new ground with gaming and the computer.

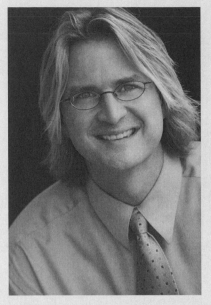

Figure CH4.1
Carl E. Creasman Jr.

I feel very strongly that gaming is now the *linga franca* for young America. In 2005, I first attempted to use gaming techniques within a EUH 2000 (Western Civilization to 1650) course. As a lifelong gamer, I agreed with Dr. James Paul Gee that the gaming industry has a lot to teach educators. The experiment was a success, though the challenges to implementation for the typical college classroom led to only a few other attempts. During the same five years, I also incorporated an immersive role-playing activity for one assessment within my EUH 2001 (Western Civilization 1650 to present) course: role-playing the Congress of Vienna. Another positive experience, being simpler to incorporate, I have continued using this learning method in that course.

For my Early American History Course (AMH 2010), which goes through the Civil War to 1877, I undertook an action research project to determine if incorporating techniques from the popular world of gaming (particularly MMOPRGs [Massively Multiplayer Online Role Playing Games] such as *World of Warcraft, Everquest, Eve,* or *City of Heroes*) would increase student engagement, performance, and retention. The main focus was really engagement and then connecting an improvement with engagement to the other two foci.

To do this, I restructured a unit within my AMH 2010 course so that students would "play the level" to complete the unit. I created five "characters" for the students to choose from, based around five thematic fields of study (war, government, culture, economics, and diplomacy) from the History field. Then I built various gaming techniques into the overall course, including the use of gaming vocabulary, grades presented as experience points (XP), formative assessments based around the character's field of expertise, and a summative assessment that utilized teamwork requiring all five characters to "defeat the boss challenge."

During the early part of the course, students were introduced to the five character classes. After a few weeks, they were allowed to choose their character by lottery in an attempt to gain equal guild sizes. (A *guild* in my parlance was all players of one character type.) By having equal guild sizes, I hoped to be able to build "supergroups" for other assessments, particularly the main unit assessment.

In all of my classes, I used a variety of classroom assessment techniques (CATs) built around student preparation. I gave students instructions about the class before our upcoming topic focus. Traditionally, this has been general in nature; for this class, I provided more development around each of the character classes. This idea of "class preparation" (what I called the daily quest for the game) was a key piece of evidence in how I determined engagement within the class. Each semester I recorded whether or not the student was prepared for a given day or not, and then incorporated that overall measure as 10% of their overall grade. It has been my casual observation that those students who were better prepared more often did better overall in the class. Some did not, of course, though it was impossible to tell exactly what would have happened for said students had they never prepared. And, equally, some students who "blew off" the daily prep, still managed to do well in the overall grade of the course, although that percentage was low.

Within the class, each day had a variety of CATs that I used to cover the material. In many courses, this was not effective because a majority of students were *not* prepared, thus not engaged in the class that day. For this course, as stated, I built the CATs to merge with the classes. Each day would see either a "super group" meeting or a guild meeting. Toward the end of the semester, there were more guild meetings, primarily because of changes to the overall makeup of the class.

For the gaming unit, I then built a special assessment that forced a supergroup to work together, just like in a game where typically you needed most of the character classes to emerge victorious. Adding to this, I incorporated a gaming ladder so that students could see instantly where they stood in the game, and therefore in the class. I also incorporated various "level bonuses" that connected to performance in the class. Most of these rewards were aids to the students that I typically gave my class, but were underused; I hypothesize that these rewards, if made more clearly and connected to achievement, would provide incentive to students.

OBSERVATIONS

Results came back mixed with no discernible impact on retention and only a small increase in overall performance. The small increase was noticeably that no student failed the assessment, unlike previous semesters. The evidence regarding engagement was more significant as demonstrated by their daily preparation for class. However, even with better engagement, the grades overall for the class, though outside the scope of the actual unit ARP, were only slightly stronger than previous AMH 2010 courses.

To start with, my withdrawals were similar to past semesters. On average, I lose about 20% of my students (across all classes); this semester it was 23% (7 total students). Findings were complicated this term because my College instituted a new withdrawal policy. Previously, students could wait until the end of the semester to withdraw in the hopes of getting a "withdraw passing" mark. The new policy put in place a "hard" date, and the professors were instructed to really emphasize this with students. I heard from several of my peers that they saw higher than usual withdrawals, especially during that last week. It is my hope that as I try this again in the Spring 2011 semester, I might see a better result.

Grades were better. Of the students taking the exam, all made what VCC considers "success"—A to C range (100 to 70 in my class), as shown in Figure CH4.2. Previously, all prior classes had some students making either a D or an F. However, the unit assessment was a different type of assessment; previously, my Unit 2 assessment was a typical exam, so comparison is not exactly fair.

Moreover, the remaining unit assessments were typical "exams" that I had given previously. A cursory glance at those student performances indicated those exam scores produced a typical grade distribution compared to other previous classes. I would need to compare those to be more accurate, but in this "gaming class," I did have a few students who made a D or F, as I typically do.

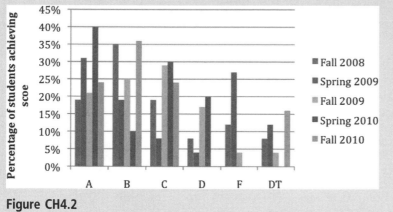

Figure CH4.2
AMH 2010 Unit 2 grades.

Of course, a deeper philosophical question emerges here about assessment. Did my new assessment adequately measure their learning for the unit? Do my older, more traditional assessments do the same? Are they too harsh? Do I grade the newer assessment, which combined group aspects, creative thinking, and writing easier? I need to think about these questions as I move into the new semester to try this again.

Overall, the grades for the course were higher, or maybe better stated, "stronger, than previous semesters." The College has a method of judging success by course, measuring students who scored a C or better against all enrolled students. Failure then includes students who withdrew. The performance was not supremely higher, but except for the Spring 2008 semester, the overall student performance was higher. Overall, my historic percentage of success is 59.86%, so the 66.7% is better (see Figure CH4.3).

But it also was stronger, or deeper. Typically in my classes, I have students who I end up curving their grade based on a variety of factors. I don't begrudge this fact, nor think it a poor reflection of those students' learning. However, for this class, I did not need to curve any students to "protect them." I did raise some grades, as before, based on my opinion of their learning, but there was no need to "help" any student gain a passing grade. In other words, due to the overall work of the semester, their grades were steadier. I attribute this to the idea of the experience Level Chart that they could see at the start of each class.

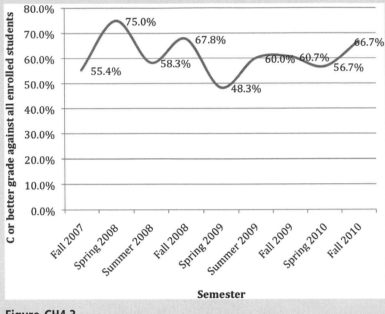

Figure CH4.3
Success rate (C or better grade).

The notion of the Level Chart is one aspect of engagement that did impact student performance, at least slightly. In previous semesters, I had been amazed at how many students simply had no idea where they stood in the course. Even this semester, I had three students in other courses simply withdraw without really considering where they stood in the class, and each was passing easily.

The idea of the Level Chart was a direct tie in to the gaming concepts. Not only did it allow students a chance to see where they were, but it did also induce a small level of competition between certain students in an attempt to do better.

Overall, it is in the area of engagement that I can point to success, though with the prior information about withdrawal and academic performance, this raises more questions than it answers. Here again, the Level Chart played a role. I think that was evidence of a very simple fact: Consistently showing students the Daily Ladder so that they could see where they stood in relation to the overall "perfect" score up to that point and tangibly see how the daily quests impacted their score, encouraged them to do the work. So the preparation work effort by the students was better. In previous semesters, the class averaged 3.69 unprepared days. This group had only 0.8 unprepared days with no student showing up unprepared more than 3 days. In previous semesters, I would have three to five students who, across the semester, did not care to do the work, often being unprepared 6, 8, or even half of the class (12–13 days).

Typically, the prep score is shown in the syllabus as 10% of the total grade. Thus, a student has to actually care enough to "do the math" to determine what their prep score is. If they *do* keep up (only a few students ever do, based on my observation over the years), they can tell easily. Most have no clue. So these students could see directly how the prep score helped them.

The only evidence that getting to choose their own focus actually made the course more enjoyable came from student comments. And while that is valuable, and we need to respect their opinion that they enjoyed the class better and liked being able to focus more on an area of their choosing, there is *no evidence* that any of that actually impacted their grade.

Lastly, engagement and absences—again, not much of a difference. In my typical semester, I see 2.63 absent days. This class had 2.3 absent days. Each class had two to four students who had high absences and so did this class.

So, low absences as with other classes, but much better preparation. Some student comments about their experience:

- Choosing my own path of study put flame to the fire in how I viewed the class. I not only was interested and happy to participate, I was also excited about the class and doing the classwork. I even started talking in class, answering questions, which is rare for me.

- I didn't feel like I was rushing through the assignment and chapter of Rev. War. I like studying specifically my topic and then taking notes on the other classes.

- I like looking at what interested me. However, some of the points were far too vague and made it more difficult than it really was.

- I got to pick a topic of interest to me, so it helped greatly to keep me interested.

- It affected my interest because I was able to study what I wanted to about history.

- My interest has been influenced because by being able to study what I enjoyed helped me enjoy history more.

- The interest of learning was not changed, but the structure of this unit made me feel I did not learn about the revolution as a whole.

- The structure definitely influenced my interest positively.

- The role-playing took it from interesting to AWESOME. I prided myself upon having one of the leading positions on the "leaderboard," which resulted in my having one of the highest grades.

- The role-playing was unique and beneficial. I liked learning about what I thought was interesting.

Some final thoughts: I guess the students liked playing the game because, after the unit, I gave them the option of keeping the gaming structure or going back to the traditional class. They voted overwhelmingly (21–2) to stay with the gaming unit. The two who voted against it were concerned about "learning everything there was to learn" in the course.

I thought perhaps the class voted for the structure because they liked the fact that I had made all extra credit more transparent. However, only three students did significant extra work, so the extra credit options were of little value or interest to the students. Two of those students "needed it" or got a bump in grade because of their efforts; other students clearly *would* have gotten a bump in their grade had they done the same level. In fact, had other students completed an average amount of extra credit work, they all would have gotten a bump in grade.

So, I suppose I can conclude that they just liked the concepts of specific topics to study, doing more group work, the ability to see clearly where they stood in the class, and maybe just the idea of being in a "game."

I have mixed feelings because, as I stated previously, the general rule of thumb is that more engagement leads to higher scores. Based solely on the math, if these students had performed the historic level of preparation as seen in my other classes, at least three to six of them would have gotten lower grades, probably a full letter grade. Yet, in each class I teach, I have some students who do not do the preparation and they make an A or B, while some students *do* the work but don't make an A or B. In fact, this class "blew the curve" in comparison because 81% of them did "B or better" in the preparation. Historically that number is about 50%.

I have done some research to see that, in general, my students who are prepared at B or better get the VCC success level (C or better grade, with 72% getting an A or B grade). And, of those who did C or worse prep, 72% of them got a C or worse. This group had 81% with a B or better prep and 71% got an A or B; the remaining students who had less than a B in prep—50% got a C or worse.

This is all hard to measure, of course, because there is no way to replicate the student being in class, or there being no overt demand for daily preparation. Perhaps, if they didn't prepare during the unit, their scores would have not been as high as they were. Of course, some students are just smart, so prepared or not, they do well. Some are weak, so prepared or not, they do not do well. Is it true that daily preparation helps you? Anecdotal information from some students says that they *do* feel as if they do better.

SECTION THREE

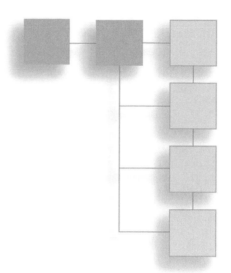

GAME DESIGN AND DEVELOPMENT

LEVEL 11

IDENTIFYING LEARNING OBJECTIVES AND STUDENT NEEDS

It's now time to examine the steps necessary to design coursework as a game. We will start out slowly in familiar territory. Video games allow n00bs to learn in a safe and easy environment.

n00b

n00b is l33t speak for a beginner, a rank amateur.

In fact, players often have to deliberately do something they know they shouldn't do in order to fail in a game's early moments. Or players may be protected entirely. They cannot do something that will harm them. That choice is withheld from them. Ready? No need to be afraid. You're already at Level 11 after all.

There are three issues that must be addressed in the multiplayer classroom's development cycle. Two are no different than any other type of class: learning objectives and student needs. One is game specific. But first, let's begin with one issue that shouldn't affect us.

HOW STUDENTS LEARN

Not all students learn the same. Or do they? Up until the 1970s, all students were taught pretty much in a similar manner. In that decade and since, a number of researchers have attempted to identify how students learn, coming up with various models such as Kolb's Experiential Learning Theory that identifies four learning styles: converger, diverger, assimilator, and accomodator. Peter Honey and Alan Mumford adapted Kolb's model to managers in business. Anthony F. Gregorc and Kathleen A. Butler based their model on how individuals perceived the world. The Sudbury model of democratic education stated that there were many ways to learn, and that each child should be given the personal freedom to learn in his own fashion. Neil D. Fleming's popular VARK model identified visual learners, auditory learners, and tactical learners.

All of these models and others have been heavily criticized. In 2009, a panel commissioned by the Association for Psychological Sciences published a report that outlined a research design to properly study the effect of learning styles, and it asserted that this methodology was almost entirely absent from learning styles studies. Of the few studies utilizing this research design, all but one feature negative findings. They also doubted the value of the significant cost of attempting to identify the precise learning style of every student over other interventions such as individual tutors. They concluded that "at present, there is no adequate evidence base to justify incorporating learning styles assessments into general educational practice. Thus, limited education resources would better be devoted to adopting other educational practices that have strong evidence base, of which there are an increasing number."

Then, of course, there has been an outcry from the defenders of learning styles and a subsequent pushback from defenders of the critique, and on and on and on.

How Gamers Learn

I am not a researcher or a scientist. I certainly am not going to step into the middle of this debate. One day it may be proven that the players of video games fall into a certain learning style, or none at all. Or there may still be some new secret to education out there we have not yet discovered. All very well and good, but it doesn't matter. Why? For the simple reason that designers of multiplayer classrooms are not exploiting learning styles or any other educational system. Video games succeed for millions upon millions of players because it doesn't matter *how* the players learn. They learn because they *want* to.

The punishment inflicted on video gamers when they fail is minor when compared to failure in the real world. So players can feel they are heroically picking themselves off the grimy floor of a dungeon to try and try again. Video games encourage players to learn and reward them, both extrinsically and intrinsically, when they succeed. That is why the range of students at Marked Tree High School in Case History 1 and at Robert Lewis Stevenson Middle School in the case history that follows this level can all be reached.

Game designers routinely tweak their games for all sorts of players. In 2005, I began the first design of three video games based on Agatha Christie mystery novels: *And Then There Were None* (aka *Ten Little Indians*). At first glance, using books where the primary action involves detectives questioning witnesses and suspects over tea in the village vicarage might not strike one as appropriate material for video games, which even more than movies and television, are an action medium. In fact, video games are the only medium where the audience is an active participant. Yet would a first person shooter be the best type of game for an Agatha Christie novel (see Figure 11.1)?

Figure 11.1
Hercule Nukem.

- You are Poirot, a murderer's worst nightmare!
- Gun down the forces of evil!
- New and unique weaponry!
- Secret Belgian finishing moves!
- Hyper-realistic character models!
- Blood spatter effects with accurate physics!
- Custom tailored wool, cotton, and silk body armor!
- All new waxed moustaches targeting system!
- Power Packs include tisanes and fois gras!
- Health bar tracks Poirot's hunger!

Probably not. However, Agatha Christie readers are puzzle solvers. Mysteries are a string of puzzles. As each one is solved, more of the truth of the story is revealed. As a puzzle in a video game is solved, the story and the player advance. As I've written in my book, *Character Development and Storytelling for Games,* action is not simply fights and car chases. "A commentator can describe a chess match as filled with action: two minds battling it out with move or countermove. A sharp exchange of dialogue in a courtroom drama is action." Knowing that puzzles were the connection between Agatha Christie and video games helped me immensely.

The important thing is to know your audience. Educators interested in trying to implement the multiplayer classroom must know their audience as well. Happily for teachers, we usually know quite a bit about our audience: its age, gender distribution, learning abilities, and so on. We also know what it is we're meant to teach. Whether it's calculus or the First World War, we are preceded by generations of teachers. The coursework is established. We not only know it for a specific class assignment, but we also know where that assignment is meant to fit in the continuum. Calculus should probably not be taught before addition and subtraction. The First World War should probably not follow World War II.

We've even been given some pointers on how to teach it. But even so, it can be a struggle. As I pointed out earlier, it's very much like writing and designing an alternate reality game. The classroom is not a hermetically sealed chamber. It is part of the real world. Time passes. Real people enter with certain expectations and attitudes for which no amount of curriculum planning can prepare us. We must adjust.

So, if we are curious enough about designing our class as a game, the first question we should ask is this: Is the material appropriate to be presented as a game? As the case histories in this book show us, we've only just begun to ask that question. But we can look at a class as a series of puzzles that must be solved by our students, whether those puzzles are explicit (quizzes, exams, questions posed by the teacher during a lesson) or implicit (how can a student take good notes?). Each assignment is an obstacle that must be conquered. It isn't that much of a reach to state that the obstacle is something from a video game: that theorem must be *crafted*; that *mob* must be overcome.

I have yet to hear from an educator who has tried to design a multiplayer classroom and discovered that nothing of their subject is suited to some form of gameplay. If there is another edition of this book, I hope that it will contain many more examples of coursework that can be constructed as a game. I hope there will be other books, and more real research concerning the best ways of designing classes as games. We are only beginning to scratch the surface.

Educational goals do not change in the multiplayer classroom; only the road we take to reach them changes. The first step is to list them as you would in any traditional class. These goals are broadly stated, and need not refer to games at all. In fact, they shouldn't. It isn't our purpose to mold outcomes to fit the procedure but the other way around.

Objectives on the other hand are specific, measurable outcomes. Here is where you identify your audience and what you expect from them. You've undoubtedly heard basic learning objectives called the ABCD's: **A**udience, **B**ehavior, **C**ondition, and **D**egree.

- **Audience.** Your audience is your students. In games, it is your players.
- **Behavior.** The actions needed to demonstrate learning. In games, it is the actions that result in a player overcoming an obstacle, solving a puzzle, completing a quest.
- **Condition.** The tools a student may or may not use and the circumstances under which the student may learn. Calculator? Open book? In

games, these are tools to create items or weapons to fight mobs—and the rule set that governs play.

■ **Degree.** What criteria will measure the student's success? In games, it can be the level achieved or the phat l00t needed for the player's continued success.

If your audience involves participants, or interested parties, in the educational system of the United States, then your goals are these:

■ Goal 1: Ready to Learn

■ Goal 2: School Completion

■ Goal 3: Student Achievement and Citizenship

■ Goal 4: Teacher Education and Professional Development

■ Goal 5: Mathematics and Science

■ Goal 6: Adult Literacy and Lifelong Learning

■ Goal 7: Safe, Disciplined, and Alcohol- and Drug-free Schools

■ Goal 8: Parental Participation

We're on firm ground here, aren't we? Nothing new or earth-shaking so far.

Student needs are as vast as their numbers. But again, they rarely walk into a classroom as entirely unknown quantities. Special needs students are identified as part of school policy. They should arrive armed with official papers outlining learning or behavioral issues that have been identified, as well as instructions on how to create the best learning environment for them.

Some students may need to pass a course because it is required by the school. Others may need it as preparation for a university, or a degree, or simply because they want to gain knowledge on a specific subject for a career or a hobby, or just out of curiosity. It's important to know why they are in that classroom. It's one of the first questions I ask.

The next question is designed to gauge their game literacy. Some students will know every game term I've used in the body of this book, and many more. Others will have played casually. And some will never have played at all. The needs of all these students must be taken into account as well. So this is the next question I usually ask on that first day.

Once we've identified our audience, written our learning objectives, and identified the individual needs of our students, it's time to make some specific decisions about our games designs. We'll tackle those on Level 12. But first, here is our next case history: a multiplayer classroom with such a range of diversity that it requires two teachers.

CASE HISTORY 5

ROBERT LOUIS STEVENSON MIDDLE SCHOOL: GENERAL MATH

Matthew Baylor

Charles Souza

Robert Louis Stevenson Middle School

Honolulu, Oahu, Hawaii

Here is the story of our youngest multiplayer classroom: a seventh grade math class. The game is *Knowledge Quest*, set in medieval times. A good deal of thought went into mapping game terminology to common classroom objects and tasks. The quest for an experience bar is heroic. I love the negative XP for not closing laptops. And there was an additional factor to be considered. This was an eclectic group of students to say the least.

As we saw with the Marked Tree High School case history, the game must reach a variety of ages and demographics. Here we have a class composed of several demographics of varying abilities and needs. A primary challenge was to design a game for a class that included a mix of students, including special education students and English language learners.

So let's journey into the past on the island of Oahu, and the class that with the help of their instructors (shown in Figure CH5.1) turned it into a Treasure Island indeed.

Figure CH5.1
Matthew Baylor and Charles Souza.

ABOUT THE CLASSROOM

Our classroom is a seventh grade (inclusion) General Math class at a public middle school in the Honolulu District of Oahu. The inclusion aspect of our class is that we have anywhere between three to five special education students who are in each class, without an aide. Because of this, there are two teachers in the classroom. Along with the special education students, we also have ELL (English language learners), ranging from barely any English to very good English.

HOW *KNOWLEDGE QUEST* WAS INTRODUCED

Robert Louis Stevenson Middle School utilizes different technologies in the classrooms, such as Promethean Boards and Google Docs. In our classroom, each student has a laptop, a TI-73 (Navigator) Explorer Calculator, and each student at the school has his or her own Google account. On the first day of the third quarter, we introduced the class no longer as a normal class but as a multiplayer game set in medieval times called *Knowledge Quest*. Using Google

Sites, we created a basic Web presence to explain the rules and also for the students to visit and keep track of their progress at *www.rlsms.com/kq*.

It started as a way to get the information of how the game worked on the first day, and it evolved daily. Google documents, spreadsheets, forms, gadgets, and presentations were all being used and were easily uploaded to a Google site. Experience points and gold were all inputted into one spreadsheet. From the spreadsheet, we now had charts linked to total XP for each kingdom, as well as each individual avatar. Each student had his or her own page with an automatically updating status bar linked to the XP page. Achievement badges were also placed on the students' pages.

The basic rules were as follows:

- Class time would be divided between fighting monsters (Homework, Worksheets, etc.), completing quests (Presentations, Case Studies, etc.) and crafting (Maintenance of Online Math Document, Use of Navigator System, White Board Work, etc.).

- At the beginning of the semester everyone in the class would choose and name their avatars.

- Guilds (groups) would be chosen and balanced as closely as possible by skill level and interests.

- Guilds would choose their names and design their shields.

- There would be six to seven guilds of three to four members each, depending upon class size.

- Students would begin on the first day of class as a Level 1 avatar. Level 10 would be the highest level they could achieve.

The first activity we introduced was to fill out an index card with their avatar's information: avatar name, kingdom shape (each period decided on a shape, circle, diamond, infinity, and star were chosen), seat number, strongest math subject, and to draw their avatar on the back. Second, we had each group of four build a Guild Crest. Each guild had four students, based on skill levels, chosen by the teachers. Each team had a high, a high-medium, a medium-low, and a low, or inclusion student, and we attempted to match personality types and students who would work best together. We did this so that each group was balanced, the lower range students had an opportunity to learn from their peers, and each group had an equal chance of winning any sort of competitions we might play during the course of the day. The Guild Crests were shields, printed on paper with four equal segments and a section for a guild name. The students were to come up with a guild name, design a logo, and color it. Once completed, we hung them up in the classroom.

The first thing to note was that the XP the students were receiving was not directly related to their grade in the class. The students still received a grade (0–4 scale) on homework (10% of their grade) and quizzes/tests (90% of their grade).

How to gain experience and level up was explained, and it was also posted on our website. Each day we had the students log into their Google accounts, open their Math Notes document in their Google Docs, and type in the Learning Goal for the day. We also had them log into their Navigators. This was worth 50 XP if every member of the guild had this completed.

Before introducing *Knowledge Quest,* some students would come in, talk with their friends, not take out any materials to work with, the bell would ring, they would still be talking and not inputting their learning goals, and some would never write down the learning goal. As soon as we introduced *Knowledge Quest* and were giving students XP for completing these tasks, over 90% of the students were in class, seated, logging into their Navigators, and filling out their Math Notes with the learning goal for the day before class even started. Many students were now putting their learning goals into their notes before school or during recess. To encourage working as a guild, the 50 XP would only be given to the guild if every member had completed the task. As a result, students paid more attention to what their guild members were doing and reminded them to finish their work before doing anything else.

Students who received a 4 on a quiz would receive 300 XP (150 if done on a retake). A 3 on a quiz would be given 200 XP (100 if done on a retake). A 2 would be 100 XP (50 on a retake). On the more difficult CFA tests (monthly assessments), a 4 would be given 500 XP (250 on retake), a 3 would be given 400 XP (200 on retake), a 2 would be given 300 XP (150 on retake).

XP was also given for progress reports. If your grade in the class was an A, you would be given 300 XP, a B would be given 200 XP, and a C would be given

100 XP. Progress reports were given out every third, fifth, and seventh week of the quarter. This was done in an effort to get students to keep up with their grades throughout the quarter and not try to complete everything at the end of the quarter.

Homework, completed and turned in on time, was worth 100 XP. We saw an increase in homework being turned in, especially from a few of the inclusion and low students. This helped their grades, but overall, they showed more interest in leveling up than what their grades were. We could count on one hand how many times students asked: "Will this help my grade?" We had shown this to be true via our Marketplace, where students could buy "items" with the gold they earned.

With each level, students were given a certain amount of gold, which, in turn, they could spend on a number of different items in the Marketplace. Students could purchase things such as bottled water, chips, 20 minutes of game time on the PlayStation in class, 500 XP, pencils, dry erase markers, bonus points on their CFA, or quiz scores (which improved their grade for the class) and also a free homework pass. So far, 64% have purchased the 500 XP, 14% have purchased a homework pass, 14% have purchased game time, and 8% have bought chips. That is 0% bought the items that would improve their grades. This told us that the students were more interested in leveling up than they were in receiving a specific letter grade for the class.

A few extra features we added since the start included:

- **Badges,** which were little images that were added to the students' account pages when they performed a certain task well, such as asking great questions, or when the entire guild logged into their Navigators and Math Notes on time for a week straight. These seemed to be good incentives, but they were also very demanding on time, as it involved updating dozens of students Web pages more frequently.

- **Bonus Quests,** which were posted almost on a daily basis and were a great source for students to earn an extra 100 XP and either review material or current benchmarks. These were posted on the website, and were submitted via Google Forms.

- **Scheduled Tutoring,** where students came in specific days during recess and received extra help, either with the tests coming up or on work they needed to redo. This was worth 100 XP. We had tutoring before *Knowledge Quest* and had seen an increase from zero students to almost six to seven students every time it was offered. From what we observed, it was stemming mostly from students who were very close to each other in total XP and were trying to keep up with each other. The students who really needed the help came in less frequently, but still more often than previously.

■ **Negative XP** for not closing laptops as they left. We introduced this due to laptops being knocked over by bags and damaged while students were leaving class. This was a major issue getting students to remember to close their laptops before leaving class, but as soon as we introduced -50 XP for everyone in the guild if anyone in the guild left it open, the number of laptops left open dropped to zero. With no reminders or any sort of incentives, students continued to close their laptops, or if their guild member forgot, another member would close it for them. On some occasions, other guild members had been closing others for them. This drastic change was one of the most surprising outcomes and sustained itself with no reminders from the teachers.

Some of the observations we made during the time we began using *Knowledge Quest* in the classroom:

■ Students were coming into class on time and were working together to complete their daily task of logging in. After they were finished, the students went onto the KQ website to see what their XP was and what badges they had earned.

■ Our original thoughts were that picking avatar names was not going to be that important, but it really set the tone for the entire project. Students also created names for their guilds, which seemed to give them a sense of unity. All guilds created a shield, which also added to their togetherness.

■ When going over what an equation was, we used a lot of gaming vocabulary. We did a weapons check, pencils were swords, dry erase markers were wands, red pens were torches, whiteboards and erasers were shields. The students, particularly the boys, responded really well to this. I did see a small divergence in boy to girl participation, but the participation by these girl students was even lower before KQ. However, the student with the highest XP was a girl.

- As pencils and dry erase markers were a necessity in the classroom, before *Knowledge Quest* students were just given them when they didn't have them. Now, students were automatically charged 50/150 gold if they did not have a pencil or dry erase marker, respectively. This led to a large increase in the number of students bringing their materials to class. Badges were also awarded to those who consistently brought all their weapons to class.

- One student in particular who had not had much success in class before *Knowledge Quest*, was now fully engaged, turning in all homework assignments, and working really well with guild members. On multiple occasions, this student mentioned that math is now their favorite subject, and it is because of *Knowledge Quest*. Their grade is still low, but they have a better attitude and have made substantial progress in class.

- After introducing *Knowledge Quest*, 30% of students who had a grade letter of C or below for the first two quarters, had increased their grades to a B or higher.

- There are a total of 107 students, split between four periods. As of March 2011, 5% were level 1 (of which four students were new to class), 28% were level 2, 32% were level 3, 20.5% were level 4, 7.4% were level 5, and .9% (one student) was level 6.

- There has been some switching of guild members due to an imbalance in skill level, personality clashes, students leaving the school, and so on. But, for the most part, the guilds in which students were originally placed have worked well.

- When students have to work in their guilds during class time, a timer is started, and we say, "Enter battle formation!" This is the signal for students to work in their guilds.

- In order to set the tone in the classroom, medieval music often is playing or is played once our timer goes off. Students seem to enjoy the music and get into the game more when music is played along with the lesson.

As a whole, the structure of the curriculum has not changed, but rather what has changed is the vocabulary and context. With a little imagination and energy, changing a classroom into an RPG of any setting or time frame is as easy as renaming pencils to swords, math problems into monsters, squares into plots of land, and perimeters into fences around your land. This has been a very effective method to engage our students and to teach them in a manner that they will both enjoy and remember.

WHY WE WANTED TO TURN OUR CLASSROOM INTO AN RPG

Turning our classroom into an RPG started after a discussion on what the motivations of our seventh grade students were. Having seen students time and time again playing simple flash games, hearing conversations about what new games were coming out, seeing students play card games on campus, and even creating their own games with "Silly Bands," it seemed obvious what the driving force behind our students' interests were. But what was it that kept them coming back? After doing some research and watching a few TEDtalks, one which mentioned Lee Sheldon's class, and others that mentioned the power of gaming to engage and promote learning, we decided to come up with a game model that would work for our classroom.

Being mild gamers ourselves and having some basic information on the psychology of gaming and other game theories, the one aspect of our game that we knew we needed to have was the experience bar. The experience bar, which fills until leveling up and then reverts back to empty, fulfills our motivating factor for a number of reasons. The tasks that fill the bar would be attainable and, therefore, would not discourage some students. The bar would be constantly growing, encouraging the students to continue their work in order to level up. Once the bar was filled, they had the achievement of leveling up, but now were left with an empty XP bar, which they once again wanted to fill up. We have experienced this ourselves with games, such as *We Rule* and *World of Warcraft*.

Our efforts to find an experience bar that was easily programmable came up empty. However, with the help of our school administrators, we figured out a relatively simple method of creating an experience bar, using Google sites and gadgets.

LEVEL 12

STUDENT DEMOGRAPHICS

As we saw on our last level, the first steps to designing coursework as a game are almost exactly what we do to prepare for a traditional class. We stray only when in the interests of knowing our audience, we determine their level of knowledge and comfort within the world of video games. We'll continue our preparation by looking in more detail at three key aspects of our possible audience: age, gender, and income level.

AGE

The case histories in this book represent a great swath of age groups from 12 to adults. Most of these adults are in their early twenties, although there are some older adults as well. Let's start with younger ages (see Figure 12.1). To do that, we will begin with an important detour.

The Entertainment Software Rating Board describes itself as "a non-profit, self-regulatory body established in 1994 by the Entertainment Software Association (ESA), formerly known as the Interactive Digital Software Association (IDSA). ESRB assigns computer and video game content ratings, enforces industry-adopted advertising guidelines, and helps ensure responsible online privacy practices for the interactive entertainment software industry."

Figure 12.1
Growing up in the Gamer Generation.

Their rating system is the video game industry's equivalent of the Motion Picture Association of America, which rates movies. Even though compliance is voluntary, almost all retail games sold in the United States and Canada are rated by the ESRB. As their website states, "Many retailers, including most major chains, have policies to only stock or sell games that carry an ESRB rating, and most console manufacturers will only permit games that have been rated by ESRB to be published for their platforms. They offer ratings from Early Childhood to Mature."

Of the 1,638 ratings assigned by ESRB in 2010:

- **1%** received an EC (Early Childhood) rating.
- **55%** received an E (Everyone) rating.
- **18%** received an E10+ (Everyone 10+) rating.
- **21%** received a T (Teen) rating.
- **5%** received an M (Mature) rating.

The ESRB is also a great source for statistics about the video game industry. I have been using the term "video game" to be media independent. However, the ESRB breaks the industry into two categories, reserving "video games for games played on consoles such as Microsoft's Xbox 360, Sony's handheld PSP, and the Nintendo Wii" and "computer games" for those games played on PCs or Macs.

Some highlights you may find useful:

- 67% of households in the United States play computer or video games.

- The average game player age is 34.

- In 2010, 26% of gamers were over the age of 50.

- 60% of gamers are male; 40% female.

- Women age 18 or older represent a significantly greater portion of the game-playing population (33%) than boys age 17 or younger (20%).

- Parents are present at the time that games are purchased or rented 93% of the time.

- Parents report always or sometimes monitoring the games their children play 97% of the time.

The occasional heated news report featuring some politician or civic leader decrying the horrific numbers of pre-teen boys wallowing in blood and gore without their parents' knowledge reveals instead that the report's subject is wallowing in his own ignorance or outright fantasy. If the children wallow, they wallow with their parents' permission or indifference. And the numbers of bloody shoot-em-ups has fallen dramatically in the past few years, eclipsed by the casual and social game revolution.

As we know, the video game industry has undergone a huge sea change in the past few years, beginning with the Wii on November 19, 2006, opening up gaming not just to parents interested in bonding or monitoring their children's gameplay, but also to parents interested in having fun themselves. Hot on the heels of the Wii came the iPhone on January 9, 2007, with a catalogue of 200,000 apps, thousands of which were casual games. And the last nail in the shooters' coffin were the "free" social games on Facebook that are played by millions upon millions of players.

Pre-teen and pre-school children do play games of all varieties; some of them most of us would consider entirely inappropriate for their age. And until the invasion by casual and social games, teachers who wanted to use educational games in their classes were faced with the fact that almost all lacked the production values of the big budget games. Now, however, production values are all across the board from cutting-edge graphics on AAA titles to simple Flash animations on Facebook.

Still, even the youngest child expects a certain level of engagement that comes from quality game design and storytelling. Whether we use video games in the classroom, or design the coursework as a game, they will notice the difference in quality immediately and punish us with their inattention.

Just as we create traditional age-appropriate coursework, so too must the multiplayer classroom be age-appropriate, and not just for children, as shown in Figure 12.2.

This new wave of casual and social games has swept up older players as well. There have been many reports of games being played in assisted-living facilities to sharpen reflexes and cognition. And, of course, family members of all ages are now playing together (see Figure 12.3).

The older members of the population make up a huge portion of continuing education students. I suspect more than one teacher of a continuing education class is playing around with coursework as a game.

Figure 12.2
Catching up to the Gamer Generation.

Figure 12.3
There is no gap between Gamer Generations.

And education does not always occur in schools. On Level 2, my focus was specifically school-based education. But corporations everywhere are using games to engage and motivate their employees. I have been approached by corporations interested in everything from improving their employees' fitness to exploring the use of games to teach safety.

Corporate executives are a very different audience from their employees, as I discovered when I created *Skelton Chase 3:Warp Speed* to encourage team-building and to introduce the concepts and hardware of transmedia to upper-level executives. These executives, both male and female, were highly competitive, very conscious of their place in the corporate hierarchy, and a few were far too eager to delegate responsibility for most of the gameplay to their juniors and then reap the rewards.

Age is a critical factor in how to design a multiplayer classroom. And even within age groups, we find different attitudes and educational goals. There are still two other factors worth considering.

GENDER

I chose the previous images deliberately to favor one gender. Another stereotype of gamers I hope we can lay to rest is that they're mostly teenage boys. Two of the most important statistics from the ESRB address the distribution of gamers according to gender. Forty-percent are female and their numbers are still growing. And there are almost twice as many women over 18 playing games than teenage boys. There are three points I would like to bring up here.

There have been a number of attempts to design games strictly for women. Yet, there is ample evidence that this approach simply creates a self-imposed ghetto for women. Men are far less likely to play games designed explicitly for women, limiting the market for such games. Some men think playing these games will make them seem like sissies, or they're angry that women are trying to exclude them. Of course, this ignores the fact that men have been making games for decades with subject matter pretty much guaranteeing that their audience will be predominantly male. And stressing over being thought of as less than manly for playing games says more about someone's lack of self-esteem than anything else.

I have always been of the belief that the most successful stories are not exclusively aimed at a particular demographic but are inclusive, offering something for everyone. Movies have known this for a long time. Animated films routinely include references aimed at the parents who have brought their children to the theatre. Chick flicks offer attractions for the males who might feel put upon being dragged to the theatre, and in the process, save them from themselves. "Well at least there's a car chase at the end of that one," they console themselves. "Maybe he's more sophisticated and well-rounded than I gave him credit for," marvel their dates.

The most beloved and successful movies of all time were written either by accident or on purpose to appeal to the widest demographic from *Casablanca* to *Avatar*. *Casablanca* surrounds its romance with intrigue and suspense. *Avatar* makes us care about its characters because they care about one another. That, plus the astounding graphics, may make us more willing to overlook some clumsy thematic elements.

So the rule here is simple: Do not design for men or women alone. Broaden the tent to include as many people as you can. They will thank you for it.

But by the same token, resist pretending that women and men all look at the world through the same 3D glasses. They don't. In games, for example, solid research suggests that men enjoy competition; women enjoy collaboration. Are there men who enjoy collaboration more? Yes (raising hand). Are there women who enjoy competition? Of course! So another step in your learning about your audience is to identify those elements that attract women as well as men and include them in your design.

Finally, despite the number of women playing games, the number making them remains disproportionately smaller by an embarrassing margin. One of the things that has pleased me immensely about the Rensselaer game program is the number of female students. Do their numbers match the percentage of women players? No. Not yet. But their percentage is growing. And their contributions to the multiplayer classroom, in fact the contributions based on the diversity of students in my classes in general, cannot be overstated.

It should be noted that one does not need to be female to write engaging, true-to-life female characters any more than one needs to be male to write male characters. The human imagination, coupled with the talent to translate that imagination for an audience, can handle both with aplomb. But we must find, encourage, and support more women in the still male-dominated careers that make up a game development team.

On the next level, I will suggest that, if you are uncertain whether you can design your own games, you will want to seek out help. We see this reaching out in action in a couple of the case histories in this book. Reach out to women wherever you can. Demand that their expertise be the equal of men, but when it is equal, give them a shot. You won't regret it. Your game will be better for it, and you'll be doing your part to help balance an inequity that has been standing far too long.

Income Level

The last key audience factor we need to look at here is income level. If there was nothing else to recommend the multiplayer classroom, here is still a reason to take the plunge. As much as Americans would like to think we are the most wired nation on the planet, it is not true. The United States ranked nineteenth in the world in broadband (high speed) penetration. And broadband penetration is now used as an economic indicator. Only 27.1% of households in the U.S. have high-speed Internet. And many other countries are increasing their percentages much faster than we are.

For example, 80% of the students in Denishia Buchanan's class in our first case history fall below the poverty line. Some schools in under-funded systems may not be able to provide a laptop for every student. And few see game consoles as a priority in every class. Just the opposite!

Even though several contributors here have mentioned using technology to supplement their classes, none need it. Neither do my own. A multiplayer classroom can be designed in its entirety without ever requiring a student to turn on a computer. Compare that to schools that spend thousands, tens of thousands, hundreds of thousands of dollars on hardware and software.

This is not to say that computers aren't needed. They are desperately needed. Our education system, once the envy of the world, has been gutted to the point where we are in crisis. And we use computers to assist in that decline, more than to arrest it. The more we concentrate on standardized tests and standardized syllabi and standardized teaching methods, the more we rely on computers to measure success, and the deeper the hole we dig.

Computers should not be used in the classroom simply to make it easier to grade multiple choice exams. But even if we don't have them to help with creativity and critical thinking, we can still give students the benefit of games to foster creativity and critical thinking—where the most technologically advanced teaching aids are blackboards, paper, markers, scissors, and glue.

Lower income classes are typically underachieving classes because standardized teaching methods fail to reach this student population. As we can see in the student opinions of Ms. Buchanan's classes—including the complaints from those students who learned biology in the more traditional way—games have the power to engage anyone.

Creating the right game to reach your audience is essential. Let's assume you now have done your homework. You know your audience inside and out, and when necessary, have researched the best ways to engage them. After a visit to Texas Tech University, it will be time to tackle the details of game design and development.

CASE HISTORY 6

TEXAS TECH UNIVERSITY: HISTORY OF HIGHER EDUCATION IN THE UNITED STATES

Stacy A. Jacob

Assistant Professor of Higher Education

College of Education

Texas Tech University

This case history makes it clear that you do not have to be a professional game designer to design a class as a game. Here all the teacher needed was to be surrounded by gamers, which is not hard these days. Highlights for me in this article included allowing students to award achievements to other students, and the use of students' avatars as a visual representation of their progress. In video games, we call this "equipping" our avatars.

EQUIP

> In video games, players provide their avatars with the best armor and weapons they can find. Not only do the stats associated with the gear make them more powerful, but it is also visible to other players, making it a great way to show off a player's achievements either due to the high cost or scarcity of the gear.

Let's see how Professor Jacob equipped her players' avatars (see Figure CH6.1).

Figure CH6.1
Stacy A. Jacob (right) with students May Lim and Ken Gassoit.

I am an Assistant Professor of Higher Education at Texas Tech University, and I teach masters and doctoral students, who are college administrators preparing for advancement, want to become faculty, or plan to work in government doing research at colleges and universities. I generally do not play video games, and I am not engaged in *Mafia Wars* or *Farmville* on Facebook; however, my husband, Jason, is an IT guy and a gamer. Over the years, he has introduced me to all kinds of games (mostly card-based like *Magic: The Gathering* and role-playing influenced board games such as *Settlers of Catan*). In many ways, I am one of the least likely persons to be incorporating ideas from a professor that is working in games and simulation arts. I like actual letters rather than emails, old books, and things from the past. Jason is fascinated with technology and loves video games. It is unlikely that I would have ever heard of Lee Sheldon without my husband's help.

About a year ago, I got an email from Jason that said, "Watch this clip, it talks about a professor who is using games in his classroom, and it sounds like a cool idea." Attached was a YouTube video of a lecture. The speaker in the lecture discussed Lee Sheldon's ideas about using gaming techniques in the college classroom. I both teach a class on "College Teaching" and am always experimenting with my own teaching. I was intrigued, so I wrote to Mr. Sheldon to ask him about his class. He sent me his syllabus, I read it, and then began thinking about my own teaching and classes.

I began talking about Mr. Sheldon's ideas in my "College Teaching" class. My students were also intrigued with his ideas, and so I started to experiment in an online class about the history of higher education that I was teaching the following semester. I created various levels that my students could achieve over the semester and a menu of assignments students could choose from, rather than a set of assignments they must complete. I also gave students choices in how they could earn participation points. The result was positive, and so that summer I decided in the fall that I would redesign my face-to-face class on the history of higher education. To do so, I turned to Jason, Jason's gaming friends, and my brother-in-law, who is also a gamer. Their collective advice, Lee Sheldon's ideas about using leveling, and lots of creativity helped me create the "History of Higher Education in the United States," a class that I will detail below.

To begin, I thought about the idea of the class being a big game with a series of little games within the big one. The big game of the class is divided into four distinct sections. I labeled the sections on my syllabus as the "Freshman, Sophomore, Junior, and Senior" years. Each year has a new set of rules as to how to earn "achievements" points and several classes within it. Each class represents a little game, which I labeled as a *quest*. Each quest has its own name based on the topic of the class. Because this is a graduate student course, each class meets once a week for three hours.

The freshman year units concentrated on introductory material to the class and contained four classes: an introduction to the course and the syllabus, two classes that overviewed the history of higher education, and a class that introduced doing archival research. After the freshman year, we looked at higher education history era by era and as we moved through the various years, like the college experience, both the history and the class became cognitively more complex. The sophomore year we covered higher education history in the Colonial era, the Antebellum era, the lead into and the Progressive era, and a class on women's education. The junior year contained units on higher education during and between World Wars I & II, and post-World War II, and student protest. The senior year covered various people who have been left out of higher education histories and modern history.

In each class, students can earn "achievement points" by doing things such as attending class, making a good point, making a great point, being helpful to others, etc. In addition to the various achievement points that I give away (in the form of various colored poker chips representing different point values), each year students also each get one achievement that they can award to any other student for things like advancing my understanding, being helpful in group work, and so forth. At the end class, I act as a banker and students can trade up chips of a certain value for better chips (gold, silver, bronze). When you trade up chips, you not only earn a more prestigious color of chip, but the new chip you pay for is worth slightly more than what you paid for it. For example, you pay 11 points for a bronze chip, but the bronze chip is worth 12 points. You have to be in class to earn chips, and you have to read and talk in class to get a chip. Even though I teach only graduate courses where most students attend and read, using the achievement points has been a great motivator to my students. This semester I have had fewer late students (mine come directly from work on campus), less absences, and much better class discussion (which leads me to believe that they are not only reading the material, but also thinking and planning for class discussion).

Students are assigned to two groups, a gaming group and an expert group. Experts pay particular attention to certain lenses in the readings each week and have the charge to do outside work to make sure they understand higher education through their lens. Some of the expert groups are popular culture, women and minorities, and government policies. Each gaming group contains different experts. Each week for the little games or quests, I can split groups out into either their gaming group or their expert groups. The expert group is a concept from the teaching literature that is generally called *jigsawing*. Group assignments for the course can also be assigned to gaming groups or expert groups.

The quests each week are games or activities that relate to the course content for the week. After a discussion of the week's readings, we do a quest to solidify the information we learned. These quests vary from a board game I made about women's history to making protest posters and chants related to class material. Some quests were created by me, and some were created by students as one of the menu of assignments from which they could choose. Students have commented to me over and over that the quests both help them remember the material and are fun.

Each student also has an avatar. It is a cut-out paper body that they drew on to represent themselves. This was our "get-to-know-you" activity on the first day of class—students introduced their avatar after drawing on them. At the end of each quest, I hand out something for them to "stick" on their avatar that represents the era we worked on (buckled shoes for the Colonial era, magnifying glasses for archival history, etc.). These are paper items I copy and cut out, and they stick on with double-sided tape. When students lead the quest, they provide the items for the avatar. At the end of the class, they get to keep the avatars as a visual representation of everything they learned.

In addition to all of this, I kept the idea of a menu of assignments from which students could choose. By using both the "achievement points" and the assignments, students can level up to a better grade. The students like it, and I like the fact that it makes every student feel that they are capable of getting to the top level, which will ultimately be reflected as a course grade of an A. If they bomb something, they can always do more, and doing more equals learning more. By using menus and leveling up, my students stayed motivated, and learning ceased to be about grades and returned to what it should be about, engaging and advancing what you know.

After my first run at the redesigned class, there were things that I needed to change, based on student comments and my experiences. I needed a better tracking system for all the points my students earned, for example. The tracking system could easily be done online through Blackboard. I also needed to refine my "achievement points" system and make it a bit simpler. Upon reflection, my menu of assignments should have been expanded to include more variety in length and type.

Designing my class with gaming in mind has been one of the most positive things I have ever done. It is lots of work and every week, I carry Ziplock bags for each student that contain their poker chips, avatars, and weird plastic objects

I give out as special awards. It is a pain, but watching my students engage in quests enthusiastically, seeing them motivated, and well prepared for class, and hearing them say that they are having fun and love history makes it worth lugging bags of things around. Let me reiterate, I am a novice gamer at best, and I am far from the most technically savvy person out there. However, with creativity, any professor can adapt a class into an exciting experience for their students based on gaming ideas. The result is a profound learning experience for both you and your students.

LEVEL 13

HOW GAMES ARE DESIGNED

Games are designed and developed. Development may follow design, or these two processes may occur simultaneously. The first style of design methodology is the traditional "waterfall" model that originated in manufacturing and was being adapted for software development as early as 1956, as shown in Figure 13.1.

I suspect you can deduce from the figure why it is called the *waterfall* method. The first formal definition of this approach was in an article by William R. Royce, published in 1970. This was a sharply critical analysis of the waterfall method, even though that word was not mentioned. The idea is simple: Start with a plan, implement it, and then look after the results.

This makes it extremely important to have a solid design document up front. Being a writer, this appeals to me. Making sure that all initial ideas are in one central location for the development team to access can save time and effort and give confidence to the development team embarking on the project, as long as they understand that the design document is a living record of what is planned, and that it will change as development progresses. Therefore, flexibility is maintained, but not at the expense of the overall vision.

However, much of the game industry has embraced a second model. Called *lightweight software development* to counter the perception of the waterfall as heavyweight development, it has been around in one form or another almost as long as the waterfall system. One of the earliest names for this approach was called *Scrum*.

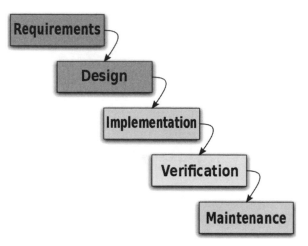

Figure 13.1
Waterfall development model.

Scrum

Scrum is a rugby term, meaning an initial struggle for the ball by the forwards of the two teams who are hunched over with arms interlocked. It's something like a more physical version of a jump ball in basketball.

It doesn't sound very promising as a development methodology, does it? Since 2001, lightweight development models have all huddled under the umbrella of "agile" development. That sounds a lot better.

Despite the complexity of Figure 13.2, it has much to recommend it as well. Again the idea is simple. The agile model focuses on teamwork, collaboration, and flexibility throughout the entire development cycle. Relying on much face-to-face interaction, agile development is accomplished in short, compact bursts from a few days to a few weeks in duration. During each of these, the steps of waterfall development are followed to produce small modules (as bug-free as possible) that, when combined, become the finished product. Agile development is often characterized by the following mantra: "Iterate, iterate, iterate!"

So okay you're wondering, which should I use? I suggest both. You're probably already using a combination of both. Even though it may feel like it, creating a new class is not as difficult as creating a new software product. And once you've done it, the next iteration of it is easier. Think of the strategy for your class as an entire development cycle highly compressed in time and space: a series of steps you are constantly revising as you work until you end up with a feasible plan of action. While you may build upon the efforts of those who have taught the class before or ask the advice of others, you do the bulk of the work. You make it your own. There is no huge team to coordinate. Even as you iterate, iterate, iterate, in the end, you have a road map for the entire class.

Figure 13.2
Agile development model.

Remember that a key to a successful game in the real world in real-time is flexibility, so you must always be prepared to adjust and even improvise where needed. This is the job of the Game Master in role-playing tabletop games.

Tabletop Games

> Tabletop games are games that are played on tabletops or other flat surfaces. Now there's a difficult definition to remember!

THE TEACHER AS GAME MASTER

You are the Game Master of the class you design as a game.

The first use of the title and role of *Game Master* was in the play-by-mail version of *Diplomacy*, originally a board game designed by Allan B. Calhamer and released commercially in 1959. It was the first commercial play-by-mail game, chess having fallen out of copyright sometime previously. In the play-by-mail version, Game Masters guided the game's negotiation phases where players formed and broke alliances as they attempted to conquer and control European countries.

Here's my edit of a useful definition of Game Master from Wikipedia.

Game Master (aka Gamemaster or GM)

> A Game Master is a person who acts as an organizer, official source for questions regarding rules, arbitrator, and moderator for a multiplayer game. The role of a Game Master in a traditional role-playing game is to weave the other participants' player-character stories together, control the non-player aspects of the game, create environments in which the players can interact, and solve any player disputes. The basic role of the Game Master is the same in almost all traditional role-playing games, although differing rule sets make the specific duties of the Game Master unique to that system.

It is important to understand that Game Master and game designer are not synonymous. A teacher need not be a game designer to be a Game Master, but, in most cases, must be the Game Master. Just as you are in charge of the development, you continue to be in charge in the classroom.

But not everybody has the talent or the skill set to be a game designer. Like any number of other creative endeavors such as writing, painting, playing a musical instrument, or teaching, game design demands a particular set of skills that hopefully work the magic necessary to create an engaging experience for your audience.

Luckily, you're already practicing some of the skills necessary to be a Game Master. Read the definition again. Couldn't a teacher's role be defined in a similar way?

Teacher (aka Instructor or Educator)

A teacher is a person who acts as an organizer, official source for questions regarding rules, arbitrator, and moderator for a class. The role of a teacher in a traditional classroom is to weave students' experience, control the non-student aspects of the class, create an environment in which students can interact and learn, and solve any student disputes. The basic role of the teacher is the same in almost all traditional classes, although differing rule sets make the specific duties of the multiplayer classroom teacher unique to that system.

Whether or not you will also take on the role of game designer is determined by several factors. Let's see how you answer the following questions.

- **Are you open to new ways of approaching your class material?** You probably will not have made it this far in the book if you aren't. An open, curious mind can take you a long way.

- **Are you a gamer?** We can see from the case histories that this is not essential. Game design shares with teachers an attention for detail, an ability to structure experiences for others, and especially important for a real world game: to be able to adjust to the day-to-day surprises that come your way.

- **Do you know gamers?** Having a gamer in the family, a spouse, child, grandparent can be a great resource. How about colleagues in your school? Parents of students? Friends at church? Chances are you are surrounded by gamers of all ages. You may just not know it.

- **Are there students you can ask for advice, or who might be able to help you with the actual design?** This is obviously more likely with high school or college age kids, but these days don't be surprised to find middle school students creating games, either with game-building programs, or even programming from scratch. It should be obvious, but just in case—it's probably not a good idea to ask students in the class you'll be designing as a game to help with the game design unless, as in my "Designing Interactive Characters" class, you want them to peek behind the curtain to see the puppeteer at work.

- **Are there any game designers on your faculty?** You'll find that game designers find it hard to say no if a new design challenge presents itself. The chance to see the design in action is a strong pull as well.

- **Are there any game companies in your area?** No, I'm not suggesting you hire a professional game designer. If you have the funds for that, then lucky you! Go for it! But you will find that game developers are conscientious members of your community who may be more than willing to volunteer their time.

- **Do you want to try it because it sounds like an interesting challenge, your students really need a change, or it just sounds fun?** You're in luck. As the case histories in this book show, a lot of your fellow teachers are giving it a shot, and having a pretty good time doing it, too!

Whether you have a team to help you, someone to bounce ideas off, or you're striking out into the wilderness on your own, it's time to get your game on.

PREPRODUCTION

There are two topics to cover first in preproduction: how much time will it take to design a multiplayer classroom, and what sort of team, if any, you will need to assemble. Let's look at time first. Part of preproduction is putting together a development schedule, complete with milestones.

Milestones

Milestones are significant points in the development process marked by the completion of a certain amount of work. (Bob Bates, *Game Design*)

The work delivered by a milestone is called a *deliverable*. If you're comfortable with a spreadsheet, use one. A three-month development cycle of a complete multiplayer classroom might look something like Table 13.1. Otherwise, a to-do list will work just as well. All you are looking for is a schedule to keep the development process on track. Do as much or as little as you think necessary.

Table 13.1 Three-Month Development Cycle

Date	Milestone	Assets	Personnel	Technology
June 1	Begin Preproduction	N/A	Designer	Word processor, whiteboard, pencil, paper
June 21	First Draft of Design	Paper design document, Wiki, Google docs[1]	Designer, Document Manager[2]	Internet access[3]
July 1	Begin Review Period[4]			
July 14	Production Draft of Design	Paper design document, Wiki, Google docs[1]	Designer, Document Manager[2]	Internet access[3]
July 15	Begin Production	Physical spaces, props, rewards, social networking resources[5]	Designer, Artists[6]	Markers, poster boards, GPS, computer, etc.
July 31	Production Complete	All assets necessary for the game, or surrogates	Designer	Any technologies needed to play the game
August 1	Alpha Testing	All assets necessary for the game, or surrogates	Designer, Testers to play the game	Any technologies needed to play the game
August 15	Beta Testing	All assets necessary for the game	Designer, Testers to play the game	Any technologies needed to play the game
August 30	Golden Master (First Day of Class)	All assets necessary for the game	Designer, Students to play the game	Any technologies needed to play the game

[1] Only necessary if design is a collaborative effort.

[2] If it is a collaborative effort, you'll want to concentrate on design, not paper shuffling. There are a lot of students of all ages out there who can do this.

[3] Only necessary if document is not paper.

[4] Show the design to colleagues, friends, or family for their thoughts.

[5] Facebook, Twitter, and so on, if needed.

[6] One or more to create props; set up Facebook page, and so on, if needed.

Whether you use the water model or agile development, having enough lead time (as we call it in television) is essential. You know how fast you usually can work on a lesson plan or syllabus, but if game design is new to you, as it will be to most who read this book, allow extra time.

I work on my own. It took me approximately a month to put together a design I thought was workable for the first multiplayer classroom. Even then, as you saw on Level 4, I didn't get everything right by a long shot. It should be clear on Level 10 that I still don't have everything right!

To keep things simple, let's say your first class will be on September 1. Start as early as you can in the summer. Do as much work as you think you need, then providing you have the luxury of time, shove everything into a drawer for a while and let it simmer. Useful editing can occur at three moments in the writing process. The earliest is *as* you write for the first time. As I've written elsewhere, "the moment I begin transferring thought to page I'm already polishing it." Allow this instantaneous editing to happen, but don't wait for it. Best is finding the right idea immediately. Better is finding it later. Worst is counting paper clips, waiting for it to happen. Even if you know you haven't figured out a design issue, or even a correct way of expressing it, put *something* down as a placeholder, even an explicit placeholder if necessary like **[leaderboard construction goes here!]**. Otherwise, you run the risk of forgetting there was an issue, and that could come back to haunt you. Even better, upon consideration. you may decide you had it all along.

The second point of optimum editing happens after you've come to a natural break. This may be a sentence, a paragraph, a section, or whatever. Your creative mind pauses, reflects. A better idea, or a clearer way of expressing the original idea, may occur. But again, don't wait. Write on.

A lot of people do a read-through the moment they've finished a story or dissertation or game design document. If you have the time, resist the impulse. Put it down, walk away, and do something else, something not so cerebral perhaps. Allow time to start to forget the minutiae of the work. Then, when you're ready and under no stress, go back and revisit what you've created. See it anew. This reading will not only generate new ideas, but it will also magically reveal typos you were blind to before.

Do you think you'll need more time than, say, winter break? Don't try and rush into this second semester. Let it simmer until the summer and then dive in. **(Horrendous mixed metaphor! Fix!)** I'm leaving this as it is on purpose. No emails please.

Time is also dependent upon team size. If you've decided to strike out on your own, fine. But if you do bring in a designer or artist or some other help, allow for their time as well. They know how fast they work. Fit that into your development schedule. And this brings up another important point. Let them do their job. I cannot stress this enough. If you don't trust the people you've asked to do what you believe they do well, and still want to do it on your own, you're trusting yourself at the same time you aren't trusting yourself. That does parse. Just think like Moëbius. Put more simply: You're the teacher. Concentrate on that job. Let your game designer do her job.

Let's assume you're doing it on your own. If you aren't, it's nice to know what everybody else is doing. Here's where you start.

BEGIN WITH THE THEME

Find a theme. The theme may change as you design. Adjustments will almost assuredly need to be made. But everything begins with a theme. And once you've found it, be true to it.

Theme
___

A theme is the central idea or message of a meaningful creation around which all else is built.
___

Your theme must be understood. There are two parts to writing, to game design—and even to teaching—creation and delivery. The best book/game/class ever envisioned is lost, if you do not reach your audience. And you must take every opportunity to reinforce that theme. The more you reinforce it, the stronger it becomes until it takes on the force of inevitability. That is something students will remember.

For example, the central theme for my "Designing Interactive Characters for Digital Games" class was this: "No matter how far removed from real life the characters we create may seem to be, they must always be constructed with the truth of reality at their core." If our characters act in a totally incomprehensible manner, with no handles that we human beings can grab on to, they destroy our willing suspension of disbelief, our ability to empathize, and therefore our interest.

How do I reinforce this theme in the class? By the scouting expeditions where the students must observe and interact with real people, asking students to revisit and refine their characters the more they learn about human behavior, and questioning how their characters react to the challenges they face in the world. Were the decisions made by the players after the debate over giving blood to the witch to save the snow leopard honest? Was it true to their characters? Or must their characters be adjusted?

Let's take another class: Poetry 101. The theme might be "Learning to understand and appreciate poetry is an essential component of a full, well-rounded and happy life, even in a world obsessed with STEM."

STEM

> STEM is an acronym for Science, Technology, Engineering, and Mathematics. STEM is an initiative that recognizes these disciplines as core necessities for a civilization to advance.

However, the knee-jerk reaction to the United States losing ground to other countries in these areas seems to be to concentrate solely on them, cutting deeply into funding for the arts and humanities. The Department of Labor has named 14 sectors "projected to add substantial numbers of new jobs to the economy or affect the growth of other industries or are being transformed by technology and innovation requiring new sets of skills for workers." None of them include a hint of music or literature or a foreign language.

Teachers are an endangered species who recognize utility and beauty cannot be at war with one another, if our civilization is to truly advance. The idea of using techniques taken from the most technology-heavy claim to art we currently have, video games, may seem ironic, even subversive, but games and gamification are everywhere. And they well may be the Trojan Horse that can sneak art and humanities into the walled fortress from which they are misguidedly excluded.

The previous two paragraphs are not simply a tirade against the trend they condemn, but an example of another important aspect of theme: It need not be universal, or all-inclusive, but you should believe in it.

THE GAME'S STORY

Let's say you are teaching a class: Poetry 101. How could this theme for Poetry 101 be reinforced? Not through diatribes like those same two paragraphs above, as part of the coursework. Some of the most brilliant and famous scientists of the past read and wrote poetry. This fruitful marriage of art and science was not considered strange in the past. It was common not much more than a century ago. And we still find this union today. In fact, the Euro-Science Open Forum in 2006 celebrated a Science Meets Poetry Day in Munich, Germany. The day celebrated the complex personality of Ludwig II, the visionary King of Bavaria. The celebration was such a success that the idea was expanded to an entire event devoted to science and poetry during the Euro-Science Open Forum in Barcelona, Spain. Factual stories like that one could easily be woven through the class to support the theme.

Or how about this? A game story could be built challenging students to uncover two secret societies intent on protecting, on the one hand, science, and on the other, art throughout the centuries. Arcane clues could be discovered in poems; strange connections between rhyming couplets and mathematical theories could emerge. And the ultimate realization for the class might be that a combination of the two could be the key to saving our civilization. Best-selling books and blockbuster movies are built upon similar foundations all the time. Why not a multiplayer classroom?

I am often asked how I come up with my ideas for stories and games, even goofy ones like in the preceding paragraph. Inspiration comes from as wide a source as the universe. But that doesn't always mean we can recognize it, even when it smacks us upside the head.

Write down some ideas for ways you could use games to teach poetry. Write down all of them, no matter how silly. (As you can see, I do.) Next, roll each one around in your mind. Try out your ideas on friends, colleagues, and family members. This will often lead to impromptu brainstorming sessions where your idea will spark one of theirs. And their resulting thought could inspire or focus your thoughts.

Figure 13.3
The Barcelona Pavilion.

While this process is in motion, consider the German architect, Ludwig Mies van der Rohe. Mies is another example of art and technology working in concert. Have a look at Figure 13.3, the Barcelona Pavilion designed by Mies. It was built for the official opening of the German section of the 1929 International Exposition in Barcelona, Spain. Meant to be temporary, the building was demolished less than a year after it was constructed. Happily, a group of Spanish architects rebuilt the Barcelona Pavilion from Mies' original plans and black-and-white photographs, completing it in 1986. This time it was built to last.

Looking at the simplicity of line and form, it should not come as a surprise that Mies is credited with the famous aphorism, "less is more." Keep this phrase in mind as you design. A common mistake students in my design classes make is to overestimate their talents and to underestimate the passage of time. Both n00bs and supposed professionals end up cutting and cutting some more to complete their games. Rein yourself in here in preproduction. It is far simpler, and less painful, than stripping away some of your best ideas because they are too extravagant to be realized.

Look around your classroom and your office, if your school is smart enough to give you one. What is already there that you can incorporate? Remember Denishia Buchanan's biology class, our first case history where the skeleton,

Princess Sodabottle and two turtles became quest givers. For two midterm preps, a hat I had on a hook by my office door became the centerpiece of the competition.

The more your classroom becomes the world of the game, the more immersed your players will be in the experience. Design opportunities to incorporate the language and trappings of games every day. And remember there is that entire world outside the room where you teach that can be reached through a computer, books, even the classroom door.

We know games are an action medium. Remember when we talked about looking for verbs we can incorporate into a video game? Gameplay is built from verbs such as run, take, climb, buy, shoot, jump, and so on. As you design, focus on what your students will do. The more your players get to do, the more they become part of the experience. In a multiplayer classroom, useful verbs to consider are answer, present, write, and so on. And as we saw earlier, these can be translated into defeating mobs, questing, crafting, and so on. The more students are actively participating in the dissemination of knowledge, the better it will be for them and for you.

This level is not intended to be an exhaustive look at the entire game design process but is rather meant to give you some ideas of how to approach the design of a multiplayer classroom. There are other books that go into game design in much better detail. You will find some suggestions for more reading on Level 17: Resources.

For now, do not forget one important fact. The multiplayer classroom occurs in real-time in the real world. That means that your game design is not done now. Nor will it be done when you've produced all the necessary assets for your game to be played. Designing the game will not end until the last day of the game itself.

OHIO VALLEY COLLEGE OF TECHNOLOGY: INTRODUCTION TO KEYBOARDING & BUSINESS WRITING, INTRODUCTION TO COMPUTERS

David M. Grimes

Information Technology Coordinator and Technology Instructor

Ohio Valley College of Technology

East Liverpool, Ohio

There are several interesting aspects to this case history. Given his mix of students, Mr. Grimes took a stealth approach to the gamer language employed in the multiplayer classroom by downplaying lingo and concentrating on motivation (see Figure CH7.1). His thoughts on intrinsic motivation, especially the idea of giving students some control over their fate by allowing them to choose crafting activities, helped clarify my thinking.

His experience presenting "World of Classroomcraft" at a conference in Ohio echoes my own experience in presenting the multiplayer classroom at the Game Education Summit at USC in 2010. Our audiences were as enthusiastic as their ideas were far-ranging and compelling. It was at that Game Education Summit where two instructors from a technical school in Texas told me that they were desperate to motivate students to come to class at all. After designing their coursework as a game, one of them said, "Now they're all coming to class. Early."

Figure CH7.1
David M. Grimes.

INTRODUCTION

The one thing I really love about "Gaming the Classroom" is that many of the components are already there and already used by teachers. It's just a matter of stringing different lessons together and changing the lingo.

After watching videos and reading articles on Jesse Schell, Jane McGonigal, and FunTheory, I saw the potential of how students and teachers could get excited, and therefore motivated, when introducing gaming aspects into the classroom. Laying the foundation from Lee Sheldon and his "Gaming the Classroom" website and forum, I was able to put together an implementation plan that best fit my students and their class needs.

EXPERIENCE POINTS

Since I have some students who are fresh out of high school and some who haven't been in a classroom in decades, I didn't want to jump full-force into a total gaming inspired classroom. One major idea I borrowed, though, was turning the point totals for class into experience points while introducing the leveling up factor.

Introducing the experience point system proved beneficial because it gave the students a path to accomplish the goal of passing the class. Going from zero points and working toward the top "A" level, students could clearly see where they started and where they needed to end to earn a top grade. By not promoting the everyone-starts-with-an-A approach, it took some pressure off the students to be perfect for my eight-week class.

I think everyone has a fear of failing and students being introduced for the first time in a college setting—whether straight from high school or from the workplace—can alleviate those reservations by knowing they don't have to be perfect day in and day out. They know they can complete assignments, projects, and tests successfully, to move up in the ranks and in the points to their goal grade.

Throughout the course, having an outline of the different levels and experience points also helped the students know where they stood every day in the course. They told me that having the experience point chart in the syllabus on the first day gave them a clear picture of where they were in the class and where they would like to be. It seemed as if it gave a clearer sense of progression through the course. The class wasn't a bunch of days filled with random assignments and tests. It became more of a journey where all the assignments, projects, and tests were intertwined and linked better.

AVATARS

Another aspect that I found beneficial was having everyone create his or her own avatar. Creating an avatar served two purposes: One, it allowed the students to have fun creating their own superhero or fantasy character on the first day. It was a nice exercise to participate in as a welcome exercise. Second, it gave me the opportunity to use those avatars when publically displaying grades, whether it was on the classroom door or on the classroom walls. The avatars gave everyone a secret identity. The Hero Creator tool was a fun and helpful tool where students could customize their own fantasy character. For the less imaginative students, a random hero chooser allowed the website to pick a hero for them.

Choice

Just like in some video games, the students had a choice of assignments to complete. In the various chapters, I always listed more than the required assignments or labs for the students to complete. It was up to them to choose which ones they worked on and finished. This availability of choice is similar to the choices that a player has in a video game. There are different paths to take, but the ultimate goal (earning an A) is still the destination.

By having these extra choices, students could pick which assignments to complete and build their experience points. I found out some students completed all the assignments, wanting to really boost their experience points or "catch up" on some points that were missed on a previous assignment or test. Some students indicated they liked having a choice of the lab activities since it allowed them to pick the ones that appealed to them the most and avoid those that may have been confusing.

Lingo

Although I did not use or stress the actual crafting, quests, guilds, or bosses lingo, I did implement those ideas and made it a point to describe that those exercises were helping the students build their skill level so they would not only pass the test, but also improve their own abilities with the computer program. So when we spent class time finishing Microsoft Word labs, like creating flyers, it was clearly understood the purpose was to develop word processing skills. When we took notes, it was also for the benefit of building upon the skill level. What we were doing was crafting, completing quests, and working in guilds, even though it wasn't explicitly mentioned.

But having the students know the reason why they were taking notes, completing lab assignments, or working on group projects did seem to provide a clearer picture to answering why we were doing this assignment or that project. Plus, it was all tied to the experience points and that showed progression.

Spreading the Word

After working with these new techniques, I became excited. I wanted to share some of my findings and collaborate with other teachers from elementary, middle, high, and upper education schools. If teachers become excited, it's easy for that enthusiasm to trickle down to the students. And that is a great emotion to have in the classroom.

In the final months of 2010, I applied to speak at the eTech Ohio Conference in Columbus. My topic was "World of Classroomcraft: How You Can Implement Social Gaming in the Classroom to Motivate Students." I wanted to share my experiences and discuss future ideas of expanding the "Gaming in the Classroom" techniques.

eTech Ohio accepted my speaking application and on February 1, 2011, I had a full banquet-style room of about 50 people interested in the topic of turning the classroom into a game.

My 45-minute presentation covered the experience point system, changing the lingo, and intertwining all the lessons and concepts to create a fun atmosphere.

The best part was when attendees submitted their own ideas. For elementary school students, perhaps having a cute monster sticker can help with the whole boss idea. The boss, or test, is trying to slow you down from beating him by giving you this worksheet. It's up to you to beat this worksheet and move closer to defeating the boss. This may help with the game storyline.

Others were optimistic in making an online class website that kept track of experience points. The idea was an online grade book or content management site with the gaming twist. The ideal tool that a teacher mentioned would be an automatic XP counter tool so that teachers could just type in a number, and an XP bar would display the total amount of points.

Then some attendees expressed optimism about gaming in general. One educator believed he could implement the gaming system into his online classroom to boost participation and enthusiasm. Another teacher thought introducing the gaming aspect could help motivate some of her special needs students as it was something that they were comfortable with and it was something that they already understood or could identify with in their lives.

Throughout the talk, I could see the gears turning. There are probably a lot more ideas that left the room that day or have been developed since eTech Ohio.

I discovered that the gaming concept in the classroom was not only useful but also fun. Students had something different from their traditional classroom settings and by offering experience points, leveling up opportunities, and creating avatars, it all promoted the key intrinsic motivation factor.

Intrinsic Motivation

During my research in finding gaming techniques for classroom use and from preparing my eTech Ohio presentation, I came across an online book by Edward Vockell, Ph.D. called, *Educational Psychology: A Practical Approach* (*http://education.calumet.purdue.edu/vockell/edPsybook/*).

In the book, Vockell lists five different factors that encourage intrinsic motivation. These factors are challenge, curiosity, control, competition and cooperation, and recognition. Intrinsic is the key motivation factor that a teacher can help instill in a student.

If a student has intrinsic motivation, it's huge. That student studies because he or she wants to and realizes its importance. That student wants to do well in school, realizing the opportunities of hard work in the classrooms. And that student will read because he or she realizes it is beneficial or even enjoyable when researching or learning about a new topic.

If you take a look at these five factors and then look at Sheldon's gaming concept, you start to see the potential in his methods. Challenge is about setting goals and working toward those goals. So, having the experience point chart, completing quests, and beating bosses all cover the challenges needed. As for curiosity, introducing the gaming concept itself stimulates the learner's interest. When I introduced options and choices for students when choosing their crafting activities and quests, it was to help students feel in control. By giving the students choices, they had more control over their learning or reinforcement on the materials covered in the class.

MINI GAMES

Competition and cooperation fit nicely into the gaming concept. Guilds can work together on group projects and other times, they can battle each other in the classroom. In my courses, I use student response systems, or "clickers," to test the understanding of certain topics. During these sessions, I will display a top point total leaderboard, only showing the top five or ten to avoid displaying low-scoring students.

After the individual leaderboard, I show the group leaderboard. From implementing this group leaderboard, I have seen students automatically help a puzzled group member and discuss the answers between themselves before submitting a response. In his book, Vockell discusses that learners like to compare themselves, but they also feel good when helping others. Implementing these mini games helped stress the competition and cooperation portion of the intrinsic factors.

Students have really enjoyed the student response systems. It's interactive, and they can work with others. Many students have expressed enjoyment in the clickers. The leaderboards brought the competition out in some students who were otherwise quiet. Students were also teaching others or explaining the answers to fellow students, which not only helped the perplexed student, but also aided in the reinforcement of knowledge in the student offering the assistance.

Personally, another mini game I like is *Ribbon Hero* by Microsoft. Instead of learning different commands in the Microsoft Office Suite, students have to complete challenges. For each challenge, say, by making a bulleted list, they earn achievement points. Even from working in the program on general assignments, they receive achievement points. These points can be posted to Facebook as well, if a student chooses to enable that option. It's a great way to diverge from the traditional lecture and practice routine when working with computer applications.

Lastly, by having experience points and levels, students can receive some sort of recognition, which is the final factor of building intrinsic motivation. Keeping an experience bar meter, congratulating on a character leveling up, or just having the students personally track their progress, offers all kinds of opportunities for recognition.

Perhaps, an XP Hall of Fame, for students who earned the highest XP levels over the years?

Link Box:

Hero Creator: *www.ugo.com/games/superhero-generator-heromachine-2-5*

Jesse Schell: Design Outside the Box: *www.g4tv.com/videos/44277/dice-2010-design-outside-the-box-presentation/*

Jane McGonigal: Gaming Can Make a Better World: *www.ted.com/talks/jane_mcgonigal_gaming_can_make_a_better_world.html*

Fun Theory Projects: *www.thefuntheory.com*

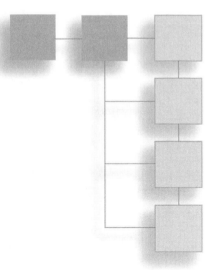

LEVEL 14

PRODUCTION

Level 13 addressed the first half of the development schedule. Up until now, it's all been about getting our thoughts in order, putting them down on paper, and if necessary, assembling the team. Now it's time to roll up our sleeves and get our hands dirty. That should be easy as we look at "Adventures in Gardening: The Game," an entirely fictitious educational experience.

But first, I want to issue a disclaimer. Multiplayer classrooms come in all shapes and sizes. Not every game you design will need the amount of preparation that goes into a video game. Video games come in all shapes and sizes, too. I've written several game design documents that were several hundred pages long. I've also written game design documents that were under a hundred pages and some even shorter than that.

While it is better to err on the side of too much preparation, particularly the first time, you can run the risk of overwhelming yourself with the project. You don't want to get so caught up in the details that the big picture gets lost. I find designing classes as games not only to be rewarding, but also much more fun to teach. Find an amount of detail and structure in the design and development process that you are comfortable with, and go with it. If you don't have fun, your students will not have fun. Keep that in mind as we dig into the production of "Adventures in Gardening" (see Figure 14.1). (And that will be the last gardening pun on this level, I promise.)

Figure 14.1
"Adventures in Gardening" classroom.

Prep

Here's the checklist of what we have already done so far:

- **Proposal** to Flower Valley Community College Adult Education for "Gardening - Beginner Level."
  - This is the third time teaching this class, but I informed them I wanted to do it as a game.
  - Idea was approved with some skepticism, in particular, whether elderly students "would take to the idea." Other comments: "might be fun" and "was worth a try."

- **Identify audience.**
  - Residents of the Flower Valley Retirement Complex

  Male and Female
  - Ages 55–107
  - Recreational facilities at the FVRC include two Wiis and an Xbox 360 with Kinect (a movement-tracking device that allows game input without a controller), so residents have had some experience with games.

- **Class size**
  - 15 registered
  - 11 women and 3 men

- **Class time:** 3–4 p.m. MWF
  - Since some of the older students tire easily, the course has been divided into three short segments of one hour each per week instead of two classes of one and a half hours each.
  - Course will run for eight weeks with a final garden party and show one month later to see how the garden has grown. Other FVRC residents will be invited to this event as well.

- **Classroom:** Flower Valley Garden Center
  - Three miles from the FVRC. FVRC will provide transportation in their bus.
  - Garden Center will donate the use of garden space and used tools with a nominal charge of $15 for all seeds, pots, soil, and so on. (Note to scout out garden center for possible awards and quest givers.)
  - Additional costs, including refreshments at the garden party and show, absorbed by Flower Valley Community College Adult Education Program.

- **After meeting** with residents at FVRC, the idea of doing this spring's class as a game was greeted with general approval. Comments: "make a change," "might be fun," and "was worth a try."

DESIGN

- Lesson Plan
  - First Week
    - Explanation of the game and distribution of game rules
    - Introduction to untilled garden space
    - Missions (quests)
      - Research the best ways to lay out a flower garden
      - Plan a garden for all five guilds
      - Lay out five plots
      - Prepare plots
      - Plant first seeds and/or bulbs
    - Take pictures and post them

- Second Week
  - Missions
    - Research families and types of flowers
      - Annuals, perennials, etc.
      - Lilies, geraniums, etc.
    - Players present research to class
    - Plant second seeds and/or bulbs
- Third Week
  - First Rewards (gloves?)
  - Missions
    - Research
    - Presentations
    - Plant seeds and/or bulbs
    - Visit outstanding nearby garden?
- Weeks four through eight continue as above

■ Decided to limit game terminology to a few easily understood concepts:
- Game Master (they need to know who is boss!)
- Leveling up
- Guilds and guild missions
- Solo missions
- Achievements
- Scouting expeditions (visiting local gardens)

■ Players will level up by completing major assignments, growing a series of flowers, each one a bit more difficult to care for.
- Players can choose among several flowers to grow at each level.
- Players can only plant one flower per class.
- If a player's flower hasn't sprouted (is showing above the soil), that player cannot advance to the next level but can plant more flowers at their current level.
- Total number of flower species possible in eight weeks: 24.

■ Players will divide into five guilds of three people each.
- To help one another
  - Differing levels of expertise
  - Care for another guild member's plants, if that guild member is unable to attend a class
- To win additional prizes

■ Players will gain rewards for achievements as the class progresses.
- Pictures will be taken to display on the FVRC Community Center bulletin board of players planting and caring for their flowers.

- Players will receive their own new tools at certain levels.
  - Gloves
  - Trowels
  - Hand rakes
- Players will receive their choice of decorative pots as rewards for precise watering and choosing the correct mulch.
- At the final garden party and show, players will get to choose their favorite flowers, whether they grew them, or someone else, to be potted and given to them for their apartments. Other residents will be able to attend the show, vote on their favorites, and purchase flowers for their own rooms.
- Special prizes are awarded at the end of the class:
  - The player whose flowers are chosen more than any others by class members wins a prize.
  - The player whose flowers are chosen more than any others by FVRC residents wins a prize.
  - The player who leveled the farthest by successfully growing the largest number of plants wins a prize.
  - The guild whose flowers are chosen more than any others by class members wins a prize.
  - The guild that leveled the highest wins a prize.
  - Others?

Whew! The gardeners among you readers will have realized I know nothing about gardening. I had the luxury of making things up as I went along. So do not copy precisely the above for your planned gardening class, or the flowers will probably never grow. But you should now have an idea of the size of that raft of ducks you need to line up before production begins. Of course, more ducks may be added, too. And yes, the collective noun for "ducks in the water" is a "raft." You really don't want to line up ducks once they are in the air. They are hard to net, and they'll usually line up on their own.

One idea that is important to consider when designing a multiplayer classroom are the types of reinforcement called the *variable ratio schedule* and the *variable interval schedule*. These are concepts long known to game designers, filmmakers, and book authors, even if they didn't know the terms for what they were doing.

Variable Ratio Schedule

A conditioning technique where responses to an action are of unpredictable amounts. In a video game, this means that defeating one bandit may result in the reward of a single coin, yet defeating a second bandit may result in the reward of three coins.

Variable Interval Schedule

A conditioning technique where responses to an action may occur at unpredictable times. In a video game, this could mean that a mob will not spawn (appear) at noon every Thursday.

Research suggests that if a player knows exactly when to expect an event, and precisely what the result of that event will be, he will lose interest. But if he is kept wondering, he remains engaged longer. This is not only a mental trait. The same behavior can also be observed in exercise regimens. If an exercise routine never varies, the body will adjust, and the effect will be lessened. Horror films use these techniques to keep their audience off balance. Book authors vary how they tell their stories.

When I teach writing, I emphasize the need to vary the rhythm of the language I use. Every word in a sentence should not be two syllables. Every sentence should not be precisely the same length. Every paragraph should not have three sentences in it. Otherwise, a monotonous rhythm sets in, and the reader loses interest.

So when creating a design similar to the one above, be careful to mix things up. Do not do exactly the same thing in the same way at the same time over and over. That's why I added scouting expeditions in "Designing Interactive Characters" and visiting successful gardens in "Adventures in Gardening." Visiting the gardens will also act as inspiration and encouragement, which is, of course, an added intrinsic benefit.

COLLECTING ASSETS

The design is ready to go. Let's continue this level as a solo quest. While you may need an employee of the Flower Valley Garden Center to assist—and you'll certainly need a bus driver—you will handle all game production.

Read through the design. Make a list of all the elements needed to create the game you want to make. That list could be in any order. It might seem best to follow the order in which the elements appear in the design document. Another approach would be to break the design into sections based on the type of activity, or where they will take place.

Choose the flowers your class can choose to plant (see Figure 14.2). Divide them into levels. Write and print precise instructions for the type of soil, mix of sun and shade, appropriate fertilizer, watering schedule, and so on, for them to flourish. It isn't your intent to hide the correct answers to puzzles as some games might do. You want to give your players every opportunity to succeed.

Figure 14.2
Beauty can be rewarding.

What is the garden center providing? A space for the garden. Establish that the three players in wheelchairs can access their plots easily. Determine that the space is suitable for five separate, appropriately sized guild plots of land that can be subdivided into individual plots for each player. Ascertain that there enough hoses, because even those players may need to share. Collect the used tools the garden center is donating, making sure they are in working order, and that you have enough for every member of the class.

Decide on the awards and prizes. Will you need to purchase ribbons? Plan shopping trips. And this bears repeating: Remember to ask every store in your community that you visit, if they would be willing to contribute to the game, instead of simply selling you what you need. I was absolutely astounded when during the second *Skeleton Chase* game a restaurant gave us all of the pizza and sodas we needed for dozens of players for free. They were a new restaurant and understood that the word of mouth created by their generosity would be the best advertisement among the campus population. Even big chain stores gave us coupons as soon as we asked.

You may have to buy a prop or two, or an award or two, but in the end you will realize that multiplayer classroom games cost very, very little to produce, especially when compared to video games.

Alpha Testing

Once you've collected everything you will need, or at least have fabricated placeholders, you are ready for Alpha. You may not have access to the garden space as yet. You may not want to disturb it until the real class arrives. Find another spot. Or even create your garden on paper. You are testing gameplay here, not the real experience. You will also not need as many testers as you will ultimately have players. There is no rule of thumb for how many testers you may need. The number is greater than one, but it may be as few as three (one guild's membership for "Adventures in Gardening").

If your testers do not exactly match the demographics of your players, you will need to study how they play, and try to interpolate their behavior more closely to match your players. If you use your kids, be careful. They know games. They will take shortcuts that the residents of the Flower Valley Retirement Complex may not be able to make.

When your testers are assembled, explain the rules of the game to them exactly as you will when facing your players. You will be tempted to give hints or guide their gameplay. Resist this! Lock your ego and your emotions away in a safe place during testing. I worked on a game that cost millions of dollars to make, but the focus groups testing it had difficulty—they were not listened to. The designers were confident they knew better. The game was barely released, and a major company was dissolved.

Instead, take careful notes and then survey your testers after the gameplay session ends concerning obstacles they encountered in how the game was designed. Find out what they thought was too hard or too easy and what gave them the most satisfaction or enjoyment. Then go back to the drawing board, adjust your design, and produce or acquire new assets. And test again. Test as much as you can—even a second Alpha test will be helpful.

BETA TESTING

The last testing period is Beta. Now there are no more placeholders, and the testing conditions should be as close as possible to how your players will experience the game. Add this to everything already discussed during Alpha testing. It still applies. Make any changes, but they should be incremental by this point, not massive.

Beta testing done? Guess what, you're ready for the Golden Master, the finished version of the game. You're ready for your first day of class. Keep your eye on your ultimate goal—what you want to achieve by the end of the course—and dive in and reap the rewards (see Figure 14.3).

Figure 14.3
The prize at the end of the "Adventures in Gardening" class.

SECTION FOUR

AFTER THE LAUNCH

LEVEL 15

PLAYING THE GAME

It's opening day. The stands are packed with screaming fans. Or, more likely, you're facing a sea of skeptical faces. Or even more likely, you're confronted with the tops of two or three dozen heads, as students surf, text, and twit, never having noticed you entered the room. Never fear, if you've gone through the extensive prep I know you have, you are ready to launch your surprise attack on an unsuspecting populace. For this populace, there will be no defense.

"Welcome to the class." Say it softly. Sneak it up on them. Now, loud and proud: "You all have an F." Tops of heads are suddenly replaced by faces. Confused, even outraged, looks are exchanged. "However, you will be able to level up by killing mobs, questing, and crafting." The confusion and outrage are gone in an instant. You see something new in their eyes: determination. And a challenge: Bring it on. You've hit the Power On button (see Figure 15.1). They are in your world now. The game is afoot.

Whether you distribute a syllabus, or simply begin to describe the game they will be playing, there are three points that must be clear, two are metagame, one is within the game.

Figure 15.1
Pressing the Power On button.

- **Metagame:** Even though this class has been designed as a game, to win it, they must acquire knowledge. And the extent of their learning will be reflected in their final level.

- **Metagame:** Explain the rules. And change them only at your peril. More on this in a moment.

- **Game:** Introduce them to the lore.

LORE

The game you've designed does not need extensive lore. It may be enough to explain what you mean by killing mobs, questing, and crafting. But we have only touched the surface of the power of narrative in creating immersion in the multiplayer classroom. As you saw on Levels 9 and 10, my current class, unlike earlier classes, is set in the fictional land of Valeria. The players are on a quest within that world directly tied to coursework. The jury is still out on whether the extra game elements, and how they are connected to student performance, will be additional motivators or distractions. But so far, so good.

Lore

Lore involves the back story of the game—everything that has happened up until now.

It's up to you. Are you somebody who slowly eases into the shallow end of the pool? Or do you dive into the deep end? Both of the approaches work. Choose the one that is most comfortable.

If you do choose to expand the lore, make sure that it is an integral part of the design and development of the game. Just as you look for every opportunity to translate coursework into gameplay, search out opportunities to reinforce the lore wherever possible.

By the same token, don't try to force lore or game conventions on elements where you can't make them work. There is a very real danger of obscuring content with the mechanism by which you've chosen to deliver it. Watch how your students fall into this trap when they do their quest presentations.

If you choose to allow your students to present class material, your role as an active Game Master is essential. I will interrupt student presentations, asking for definitions, challenging their assumptions, and clarifying important points. These are meant to be quests after all. And quests are designed as a string of obstacles players must overcome.

So, by all means, go for as many trappings of an actual game with which you feel comfortable. Keep your balance. One of the primary challenges in game design is balance. It shows up everywhere from the power of the player vs. adversaries to the difficulty of puzzles to the balance between story and gameplay. It can be the difference between hitting a home run and striking out. Maintain balance in all elements of your multiplayer classroom.

RULES

Rules for playing the game are as obvious a part of the design as the rules that govern our classrooms. Some come to us from government or the institution for which we work. Others we create. Students expect rules. They want rules, no matter how much they may complain or test them. Whether written down formerly in a rubric, or not, they want rules that are clearly stated.

Remember the midterm prep guild PvP in the "Designing Interactive Characters" class? I changed the rules on the fly. Because the students were involved in the decision, it passed without incident. They are never too far from concern about their academic progress. But if they are invested in the game, and understand that sometimes adjustments must be made, the situation is very much like on the playground when kickball boundaries need to be adjusted, or when classes must be postponed on snow days. They are used to it. And in the latter example, they probably won't mind it at all.

Scoring

Maybe it's just me, but I find grading papers to be one of the least attractive chores a teacher faces. Yet, depending upon how you've designed your game, it becomes even more important. Players expect video games to provide a running tally of their progress. Whether you use a leaderboard, or rely simply on a level and XP table in the syllabus, your students will want to know where they stand. Therefore, and this is the task I'm worst at, you cannot put off your grading.

Particularly in my current class, I'm trying desperately not to get too far behind, because how students do on their assignments will affect the narrative of the game. New pronouncements from the mysterious being who has summoned their avatars to the tower somewhere beyond the mountains to the west must be held up until grades from certain assignments are in. Even without that explicit tie between performance and story, it's imperative to emulate as much as possible the reward system of a video game. We can't match it precisely because in a video game the tally is immediate, but we must try to be as responsive as possible to their achievements.

A couple of the case histories in this book describe how accomplishments are announced regularly, say before the beginning of each class. This is exactly right. Your gamers expect it.

Staying Flexible

Rules aren't the only thing that will change during the course of the class. Outside forces are capricious. Weather doesn't care that you're supposed to teach on a certain day. Snow will fall regardless. The flu can sideline large numbers of players all at once. Quest presentations may run long. Even positive occurrences, such as a prominent visitor in your field who has stopped by unexpectedly, can throw off your carefully constructed schedule.

The first two *Skeleton Chase* alternate reality games were designed to improve health and fitness in the students who played (see Figure 15.2). The third iteration, *Skeleton Chase: Warp Speed*, reduced the playing time from seven weeks to two and a half days. The players were now corporate executives. The goals of the game were team building and introducing them to new technologies. These executives on the whole were not all that keen about physical exercise, so much of the gameplay had to be reinvented on the spot.

Figure 15.2
Rain falls on the climactic night of the first *Skeleton Chase* ARG.

But the multiplayer classroom is the real world in real-time. Stuff happens. During our first running of *The Skeleton Chase*, we had received permission from the IU Student Union to use a boardroom high up in the tower. We created a lair for one of the game's characters, a demented graduate student who was squatting there illegally. One intricate puzzle took players all over campus until they reached the room and discovered the props we'd arranged there to indicate he was camping out in the room: a sleeping bag, fast food wrappers, and five empty liquor bottles that figured in another puzzle, as well as echoing what they were learning in class that week about addiction.

A few hours after the puzzle went live, our "Game Central" hotline, manned during the set times every day that the game was running, received a phone call from the first team to find the boardroom. Unfortunately, there was no indication of the lair they had expected to find there. The Game Master on duty, Elizabeth, confirmed the props were indeed missing (the team of players had wandered off by then), and contacted the Student Union office to learn that they had neglected to notify the janitorial staff of our game. Elizabeth hurried to the union and, guided by the office, tracked down the janitor responsible for cleaning the room. Luckily, he still had all our carefully collected props in a bag on his cart.

But the janitor thought the young woman who wanted them returned was, in fact, the drunken squatter living there. Elizabeth finally managed to convince him that it was all for a game, and that it had been cleared by the Student Union in advance. He finally handed over the bagful of props, still somewhat suspicious. She restaged the boardroom, returned to the office we were using as Game Central, and called the players to let them know that the bug was fixed, and the game was rebooted. They were now free to visit the lair.

Elan Lee is one of the founders of 42 Entertainment, creators of some of the most famous alternate reality games such as *The Beast* (a promotion for the Steven Spielberg film *A.I.*) and *i love bees* (a promotion for the video game *Halo 2*). He has dozens of stories to tell about designing and redesigning on the fly. One of my favorites involves a device that players were required to build. The plan was that a number of pieces of this device would be scattered around the world, and one would even be buried in Antarctica during the winter. Since that piece, necessary to complete the device, could not be recovered for several months, designers felt they would have plenty of time to refine their design for the rest of the game and get way ahead of their players.

Unfortunately, the players contacted a scientist based near the coordinates where the object was buried. She was able to find it, happened to have a 3D imaging copier, and sent a perfect electronic plan of the piece to the players so that they could construct a mock-up and complete the device's construction months too soon. Imagine the flexibility and frantic scrambling that induced in the designers.

Hopefully, you will never have to do that much running around or explain your drinking habits. You will discover, however, that no matter how well you've planned and tested, tweaking will be necessary. I would guess you've faced similar situations—for example, when students have challenged a test question—so don't worry too much about it. Just be prepared. It will happen.

The key is to be flexible. Expect the unexpected. Modify. Fine-tune. Have a backup plan, if possible. But even if you don't, be prepared to be creative in real-time as all of those expectant, engaged players stare at you. For me, these are some of the most invigorating design challenges I've faced. And I firmly believe that if you've done your homework up front, you know the game better than anyone in that classroom. You will find an answer that may be even better than what you had originally planned.

POSTMORTEM

Yes, believe it or not, it's true, the class is almost over. Now comes your opportunity to listen and learn. Video game developers have borrowed a term from forensic pathology to describe this final step in the life of a game. It's been released. Players have played it and reacted. Critics have weighed in. Sales trends are clear. All that remains is reflection.

Decisions that were made are re-examined. Results are appraised. And the canny game designer is one who learns from the past in order to do better in the future. I'm willing to bet you may want to design another class as a game, or at least repeat the one just completed. The experience hopefully has been as much fun for you as it has been for me.

My last day of class has always been a postmortem. I take a pen and a pad of paper, and I ask the students to weigh in on their experience. You've seen the results of this throughout the stories of multiplayer classrooms that I've shared with you. I've learned more from these postmortems than I did from the formal teacher evaluation sheets the student filled out. Some of their suggestions worked well; some not so well. But all were worth considering, because they came from my players.

You will probably have specific questions of your own. Did you like the awards? Were the quest presentations fun to do? Do you think you learned as much from presentations given by your peers, as you would have from a teacher?

One more thought concerning game balance. I was surprised that a number of students in a couple of classes, while they enjoyed the presentations of their peers, wanted to hear more from me: the expert in the room. So I adjusted and became more proactive during presentations, asking questions, filling in the blanks.

I would not have had the knowledge to make that modification without a postmortem (see Figure 15.3). It is one last industry practice that I recommend to you. Students can be less than diplomatic at times. Don't let that dissuade you. Explain what your intent was, ask questions to clarify their suggestions, but don't try to argue your side. This isn't a debate. Defend your choices, and they will stop critiquing, but you will stop learning.

Figure 15.3
Feedback from the players.

As I mentioned way back on Level 1, there are three acts to a chess game: opening, middle game, and endgame. Our board is almost cleared of pieces. The story of the game is almost through. All that remains is a peek at possible futures and some resources to help you create your own multiplayer classroom.

Case History 8

Waunakee Community High School: Computer Science Classes

Aaron Pavao

Math and Computer Science

Waunakee Community High School

Waunakee, Wisconsin

One of the best innovations to the multiplayer classroom described in the case histories was the use of achievement points. You are about to see an extremely well-worked out example. Tracking these achievements on the course wiki is terrific as well. The more we publicize our students' achievements, the more they take pride in them. The intrinsic reward is priceless.

The testing method is a fascinating example of allowing the students to learn by failing in repeated "attacks on the boss mob," here embodied in the instructor.

This is the last of the case histories. It was my hope that in sharing my experiences designing the multiplayer classroom that I would challenge other teachers to come up with even better ideas. All of these case histories, even some we could not include in the book, have inspired me, as I hope they have you.

OVERVIEW

Following in the footsteps of Lee Sheldon, I have restructured my high school computer science courses as a game (see Figure CH8.1). At the time of this writing, the plan is still in its first year of implementation, so I am hesitant to draw any conclusions as yet. That said, there are certain trends that are emerging that I will include in this report.

Figure CH8.1
Aaron Pavao.

My original intent was to structure the courses as a game, with four-player (student) teams. Players earn experience points for taking tests, completing projects, contributing to the course wiki, and other tasks. Rather than use Sheldon's direct level-to-grade system, I would use a set of levels that were each worth an increasing amount of experience points, much the way any role-playing game works. Each student's grade would be based on his or her level. Each progress or grade report would compare the level to a "perfect" level for that grading period, with the "perfect" level increasing with time. Single-semester courses were to go up to Level 40, and full-year courses run to Level 80.

In addition to computer science concepts, I teach the students to work together, helping one another toward a common goal. During the first semester course, students started in groups of three or four, then merged into groups of six to eight, and finally worked as a single, organized team working on different parts of a larger challenge toward a common goal.

EXPERIENCE POINTS AND LEVELS

One of the things that struck me about Sheldon's system was that the goal was set before the game began. The students had a goal and a means of achieving that goal. Additionally, the students gained points in the class, in contrast to courses where they started with a perfect grade and watched it slip over the course of the semester. When I told students new to the computer science program that they were starting with an F as "level zero newbies," I most often saw a look of determination rather than despair.

Immediately after implementing the system, I was struck that an exponential system would be a better draw than a linear one. Players would gain levels quickly at first, getting drawn into the sense of achievement, pulling them that much further toward each level. However, I ran into trouble when making the system compatible with the district's standard 10-point grading scale. While the level would appear to comply with the standard, the actual number of experience points would not. As a result, I chose to use a linear system, rather than an increasing one.

Each grading period (two progress reports, a quarter grade, and a semester grade) had targets based on the level each course should reach by the end of that period if they had a perfect record. Each student's grade was based on how close he or she came to this target level. This was mainly achieved by earning experience points. Students could also gain "bonus" experience points, points that were not included in the target calculation, for winning competitions, helping other students, contributing to the course wiki, and the like.

ACHIEVEMENTS

One of the first things that students requested was an achievement system, similar to those of Xbox Live or the trophies on the PlayStation Network. We now have a set of achievements that are co-curricular. Achievements are not required of the class and are intended to promote additional challenge, best practices, and good citizenship. Examples include the following:

- **Ace:** Ace a test on the first try.
- **Ace of Aces:** Ace five tests.
- **Achievement X:** Get 10 other achievements.
- **Advanced Person:** Take the AP Computer Science test.

- **Code Poet:** Reach Level 40 in Computer Science II.

- **Deliverator:** Complete all Lesson 3 labs and the Pizza Order Form optional lab.

- **Elite Coder:** Reach Level 80 in AP Computer Science.

- **Fast Talker:** Be part of the first team to complete the Communication Challenge in Computational Thinking.

- **Flawless Victory:** Hit the master level at the end of first or third quarter.

- **Jack of All Trades:** Complete and pass every computer science course.

- **Journeyman:** Reach Level 40 in Computer Science I.

- **Master of All Trades:** Collect the Code Poet, Elite Coder, Journeyman, and Mastermind achievements.

- **Mastermind:** Reach Level 40 in Computational Thinking.

- **Parental Advisory:** Parental unit attends parent-teacher conferences for computer science.

- **Rapunzel:** Tallest tower in the Marshmallow Tower Challenge in Computational Thinking.

- **Sweet Hack:** Impress Mr. Pavao with something.

- **Wikilluminary:** Make five good pages on the course wiki.

- **Wumpus Hunter:** Complete all Lesson 7 labs and the Hunt the Wumpus optional lab.

I also purchased a 1" button maker and created a button design for each achievement. Students who earn an achievement are given a button and have their name put on the course wiki on the page for the specific achievement. Students have taken to displaying their achievements on the straps of their backpacks.

The display of achievements is not the only way that students have become involved. Students created a wiki page that assigned titles to each of the 40 levels of the single-semester courses. They also implemented a "prestige" system for students who completed one course and then started again at Level 0 in another course.

The list of achievements expands as the computer science program expands, and as students or I have a new idea for an achievement. I am also looking for ways to link achievements to other reward systems, such as Microsoft's achievement points or the local game stores' promotional program.

TESTING

I also modified Sheldon's test-as-boss-fight idea. In my classes, the only way to complete a test is when that test is perfect, and the student is given a number of "hearts" to complete the test.

Each time they come up during a test for corrections (metaphorically facing the boss monster), any incorrect answers cause "damage," taking away hearts, which are crossed off from their test sheet. The loss of each heart reduces the experience point value of the test, starting with 1% of the full value and increasing with each heart. The minimum value of a test that is (eventually) completed perfectly is 60% of the full value.

The "damage" of submitting an imperfect test is based on the "weapons" they use: one heart base, plus one for taking the test in teams, plus one for using their notes. Additionally, students who take their test in a team can send only one member to be graded (called a "tank" by one student), thereby spreading the "damage."

Additionally, I offer a bonus to teams based on how well their teammates do on their tests. The intent was to use social pressure to persuade students to help and encourage one another. Unaccustomed to this sort of behavior, students present this mutual reinforcement slowly, but it does emerge.

EXCLUDED CONCEPTS

In creating this program, there were a number of things I did *not* want to include. I did not want to give awards for expected behaviors. For example, I do not offer any achievement or experience points for attendance, as this is expected of high school students. Likewise, good classroom conduct is not rewarded with experience points.

Another important feature is that experience points, once awarded, would never be taken away. This design principle is in accordance with recent research that demonstrates that humans become irrational when it comes to losing something they have.

I also wanted to avoid direct competition that would have a negative impact on experience points, which is to say student grades. In this I followed the model found in player-versus-player competition in massively multiplayer games like *City of Heroes* and *World of Warcraft*, where the victors might gain the spoils, but the conquered take no penalty. This is done through bragging rights, achievements, and bonus experience points.

I also eschewed the idea of leaderboards. The idea is not entirely without merit, but not all students have a competitive spirit, and I prefer my courses to be accessible to as many students as possible. That said, students have created leaderboards on their own initiative, using them to track and rank level, test performance, achievements, and other sundry categories related directly or indirectly to their courses.

CONCLUSIONS

This is the first year of this particular curriculum. At the time of this writing, one-and-a-half semesters into the program, it is too early to responsibly offer any real conclusions. Even so, we can make a few comparisons with previous years.

The first and most pronounced differences are the increases in attendance and grades. Another marked difference is that students are coming to me to make up missed work on their own volition, rather than needing their parents to urge them to do so or to advocate for them.

Another result has been an increase in enrollment in computer science classes for both the second semester of this year and for the following academic year. The first course in the computer science series is at capacity, and higher-level classes have likewise increased in enrollment.

The ancient deities of unintended consequences never sleep, and this program has not been immune to their attentions. The combination of this curriculum and modern real-time online grade reporting has resulted in each student's grade being reported as an F for most of the grading period. I have received a number of calls and email messages from parents who see the grade report and call to ask how their children can be failing right at the start of the semester. I have included a detailed description of the program for parents and intend to record a descriptive video as well.

SECTION FIVE

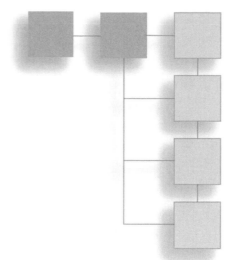

AFTER THIS BOOK

LEVEL 16

DESIGNING THE FUTURE

Lately, there's been a lot of mention of the *gamification* of society in the media. Expect a lot more. But I've only mentioned that word a couple of times in this book. That's because the multiplayer classroom existed before that word was coined. And I began to write this story about it before I had ever heard the word. But the fact that the ideas of levels and points and yes, phat l00t, are deluging us like a perfect storm, is no coincidence. The gamer generation has driven the success of everything from smart phones to the movie *Avatar*. So it should be no surprise to anyone that gamification has already been co-opted by sales and marketing.

Way back on Level 2—when we looked at *Quest to Learn* for 6–12 grade kids—I mentioned in passing an idea taking root at Rochester Institute of Technology. Last month at the Game Developers Conference in San Francisco, Andrew Phelps, the Director of the School of Interactive Games & Media at RIT, told me their dream about designing the entire undergraduate experience as a game. That's right: four years. Think Joseph Campbell's hero's journey. Last week, I visited them. They are heavily into the planning stages. Have a look for yourselves at *thinkplay.rit.edu*. And keep your eyes peeled for more innovative ideas that bring games and education together. If that sounds too painful, then just keep your eyes open. There are lots more yet to come.

Video game degree programs are turning up at universities all over the world (see Figure 16.1). There are over 250 in the United States alone, 150 submitted applications to be included in the Princeton Review's top 15 of undergraduate programs, and this year graduate programs were judged as well. High schools and middle schools are adding video game classes, and even younger students are making games in classes that otherwise have nothing to do with video games.

Figure 16.1
The future is a story with no end.

I'm not going to make predictions about whether gamification takes over the world, or whether it's already a bubble about to burst. I have no idea, and I don't really care. As long as attendance is up, as long as grades are up, as long as students who skipped class are now coming early, the multiplayer classroom is not going away anytime soon.

Enough about the past. Let's turn our eyes to the future.

In 2007, my colleague, Edward Castronova, whom I've mentioned before, wrote a provocative book, *Exodus to the Virtual World*. In it, he argues that the real world may begin to model its institutions on games because, as Raph Koster, author of *A Theory of Fun*, says, "The general populace finds them more fun." It's a future that Jesse Schell was rabble-rousing about in his DICE talk. Would our world be a better place if a primary advisor and strategist to our leaders were a game designer? I'm inclined to think so. But then I'm prejudiced.

In a book just published, *Reality is Broken: Why Games Make Us Better and How They Can Change the World*, Jane McGonigal suggests much the same thing, adding that it is game designers' responsibility to change the world, not just create fictional ones.

In my own book, *Character Development and Storytelling for Games*, I wrote about game writers and designers, "If we're lucky, we might make something more; a game that endures; something fine that we had a part in creating that will touch the hearts and minds of generations unborn. Anything is possible. The important thing is to have the will to try."

I was attempting to rally my peers and the next generation of writers and designers entering our world to make meaningful games. Now I find myself asking the same questions about our place in the real world. Teaching has encouraged me to look at the real world, and designing classrooms as games has made me very aware of the place games are coming to occupy in it.

I don't have any earth-shaking pronouncements on the level of those I cite above. I'll confine myself to this one, very important corner of the future: our children.

Here in no particular order is how I see the multiplayer classroom's future. Where is my crystal ball? Ah, here it is. I know it's just a prop from *Skeleton Chase 2: The Psychic* (which should explain partially at least the skeletal hand), but I'm going to gaze into its depths and make a few predictions (see Figure 16.2). I've written both games and TV shows about psychics. I should know how to operate this thing. Let's see. Where is the Power On button?

Ah . . . there it is . . . pushing the button . . . the crystal ball is clearing . . . I see . . .

- Researchers obtaining grants to study the efficacy of the multiplayer classroom.
- Research bearing out Marie-Pierre Huguet's observations on Level 8. The benefits are proved to be real, demonstrable, and repeatable.
- There will be more books examining classes as games.
- There will be a backlash against the concept, calling it frivolous and fleeting.

Figure 16.2
A prop from a game, but I'm sure it can be useful in the real world, too.

- Teachers will discover they can use the ideas in this book and elsewhere to design classes on their own.

- Classes as games will appear even in remote locations where computers are scarce. As I've pointed out more than once: The multiplayer classroom is not expensive. The cost/value ratio would make an accountant salivate.

- Teachers in every country will experiment with better and better versions of the multiplayer classroom (see Figure 16.3). We're currently only in Beta.

- The Golden Master will be something very special indeed.

I know. Like I said, not earth-shaking. The story is, of course, not over, but this small part of it is now complete. It is not a dissertation or a scholarly tract of any kind. It is simply a story, a chronicle of my experiences and those of others in a growing group of educators who are discovering that games are not for only the very young. We all can learn from them. When we do, the child within us can never die. Its curiosity and its sense of wonder are what keep us growing and questing.

Figure 16.3
The child in each of us must never die.

Thank you for coming along on this quest with me.

Lee Sheldon

Associate Professor

Co-Director Games and Simulation Arts and Sciences

Rensselaer Polytechnic Institute

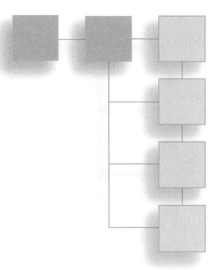

LEVEL 17

RESOURCES

Here is a list of resources in alphabetical order guaranteed to prepare you for your dive into the world of games, or guaranteed to help you keep your head above water, if you've already splashed down. Some are how-to books on game design, since we've only dipped our toes in the previous levels here. There are also books on game studies. Other resources are general introductions to what people are up to right now using a wide variety of games in education: a good supplement to Level 2. You'll also find fascinating glimpses of our future with games in it. Finally, there are short lists of prominent game conferences and organizations. This is not meant to be an exhaustive list by any means, but it will hopefully help, challenge, and inspire you. All are excellent flotation devices. Take advantage of them!

MEDIA

Each of these books approaches its subject differently, but all cover the basics and more. Also check your local continuing education and summer school programs. Classes on game design are popping up all over.

How to Succeed in Game Design

Bartle, Richard. *Designing Virtual Worlds*

Bates, Bob. *Game Design*

Brathwaite, Brenda and Schreiber, Ian. *Challenges for Game Designers*

Fullerton, Tracy. *Game Design Workshop: A Playcentric Approach to Creating Innovative Games*

Rouse, Richard. *Game Design: Theory and Practice*

Salen, Katie and Zimmerman, Eric. *Rules of Play: Game Design Fundamentals*

Schell, Jesse. *The Art of Game Design: A Book of Lenses*

Schuytema, Paul. *Game Design: A Practical Approach*

Applied Games (aka Serious Games)

Annetta, Leonard (Ed.). *Serious Educational Games: From Theory to Practice*

Bergeron, Brian. *Developing Serious Games*

Michael, David and Sande Chen. *Serious Games: Games that Educate, Train, and Inform*

Related to Game Design (Game Designers Read These Books)

Campbell, Joseph. *The Hero with a Thousand Faces*

Huizinga, Johan. *Homo Ludens*

Koster, Raph. *A Theory of Fun*

Writing Games

Aristotle. *Poetics*

Egri, Lajos. *The Art of Dramatic Writing*

Sheldon, Lee. *Character Development and Storytelling for Games*

About Games

Bogost, Ian. *Persuasive Games: The Expressive Power of Video Games*

Jones, Gerald. *Killing Monsters: Why Children NEED Fantasy, Super Heroes, and Make-Believe Violence*

Juul, Jesper. *A Casual Revolution*.

About the Future

Castronova, Edward. *Exodus to the Virtual World*

McGonigal, Jane. *Reality Is Broken: Why Games Make Us Better and How They Can Change the World*

Schell, Jesse. *Design Outside the Box* (*www.ted.com/talks/jesse_schell_when_ games_invade_real_life.html*)

CONFERENCES

DICE Summit (*www.dicesummit.org*)

Game Developers Conference (includes Serious Games Summit) (*www.gdconf. com*)

Game Education Summit (*www.gameeducationsummit.com*)

Games for Change (*www.gamesforchange.org*)

Games for Health (*www.gamesforhealth.org*)

ORGANIZATIONS

Academy of Interactive Arts & Sciences (*www.interactive.org*)

International Game Developers Association (including the Game Education SIG) (*www.igda.org*)

INDEX